Congressional
Research
Service

Commerce, Justice, Science, and Related Agencies: FY2014 Appropriations

Nathan James, Coordinator
Analyst in Crime Policy

Jennifer D. Williams, Coordinator
Specialist in American National Government

John F. Sargent Jr., Coordinator
Specialist in Science and Technology Policy

November 4, 2013

Congressional Research Service

7-5700

www.crs.gov

R43080

Summary

On March 26, 2013, President Obama signed into law the Consolidated and Further Continuing Appropriations Act, 2013 (P.L. 113-6). The act provides a total of $60.638 billion for Commerce, Justice, Science, and Related Agencies (CJS). This amount includes $7.726 billion for the Department of Commerce, $27.305 billion for the Department of Justice, $24.737 billion for the science agencies, and $870.1 million for the related agencies.

On April 10, 2013, President Obama submitted his FY2014 budget to Congress. The Administration requests a total of $63.310 billion for the agencies and bureaus funded as a part of the annual Commerce, Justice, Science, and Related Agencies (CJS) appropriations bill. The Administration's request includes $8.596 billion for the Department of Commerce, $28.405 billion for the Department of Justice, $25.347 billion for the science agencies, and $962.1 million for the related agencies.

On July 17, 2013, the House Committee on Appropriations approved its version of the FY2014 CJS appropriations bill (H.R. 2787). The committee recommends a total of $58.601 billion for the CJS agencies and bureaus. The bill includes $7.544 billion for the Department of Commerce, $26.658 billion for the Department of Justice, $23.599 billion for the science agencies, and $800.5 million for the related agencies.

On July 18, 2013, the Senate Committee on Appropriations approved S. 1329, the Commerce, Justice, Science, and Related Agencies Appropriations Act, 2014. The committee recommends a total of $63.586 billion for CJS. The bill includes $8.679 billion for the Department of Commerce, $28.503 billion for the Department of Justice, $25.442 billion for the science agencies, and $962.1 million for the related agencies.

On October 16, 2013, the Senate passed H.R. 2775 with an amendment that, in part, provided interim continuing appropriations for the previous fiscal year's projects and activities. Later that same day, the House agreed to the Senate amendment to H.R. 2775. The Continuing Appropriations Act, 2014 (P.L. 113-46), was signed into law on October 17, 2013. The act continues FY2013 appropriations (post-sequestration) for the CJS agencies and bureaus until January 15, 2014, or whenever the FY2014 CJS appropriations bill is signed into law.

This report will track and describe actions taken by the Administration and Congress to provide FY2014 appropriations for CJS accounts. It also provides an overview of FY2013 appropriations for agencies and bureaus funded as a part of the annual appropriation for CJS.

The FY2013-enacted and the FY2014-requested appropriations were taken from S.Rept. 113-78. The amounts recommended by the House Committee on Appropriations were taken from H.Rept. 113-171 and the amounts recommended by the Senate Committee on Appropriations were taken from S.Rept. 113-78.

Contents

Tables

Contacts

Introduction and Overview

This report will track and provide an overview of actions taken by the Administration and Congress to provide FY2014 appropriations for Commerce, Justice, Science, and Related Agencies (CJS) accounts. It also provides an overview of enacted FY2013 appropriations for agencies and bureaus funded as a part of the annual appropriation for CJS. The FY2013-enacted and the FY2014-requested appropriations were taken from S.Rept. 113-78. The amounts recommended by the House Committee on Appropriations were taken from H.Rept. 113-171 and the amounts recommended by the Senate Committee on Appropriations were taken from S.Rept. 113-78.

FY2014 Appropriations

For FY2014, the Administration requests a total of $63.310 billion for the agencies and bureaus funded as a part of the annual CJS bill. The Administration's request includes $8.596 billion for the Department of Commerce, $28.405 billion for the Department of Justice, $25.347 billion for the science agencies, and $962.1 million for the related agencies.

On July 17, 2013, the House Committee on Appropriations approved its version of the FY2014 CJS appropriations bill (H.R. 2787). The committee recommends a total of $58.601 billion for the CJS agencies and bureaus. The bill includes $7.544 billion for the Department of Commerce, $26.658 billion for the Department of Justice, $23.599 billion for the science agencies, and $800.5 million for the related agencies.

On July 18, 2013, the Senate Committee on Appropriations approved S. 1329, the Commerce, Justice, Science, and Related Agencies Appropriations Act, 2014. The committee recommends $63.586 billion for CJS. The bill includes $8.679 billion for the Department of Commerce, $28.503 billion for the Department of Justice, $25.442 billion for the science agencies, and $962.1 million for the related agencies.

Prior to the beginning of FY2014, congressional action occurred on an interim continuing resolution (CR) that would have provided continuing appropriations for projects and activities for which authority existed during the previous fiscal year.[1] H.J.Res. 59 was introduced on September 10, 2013, and passed the House on September 20. On September 27, the Senate passed H.J.Res. 59 with an amendment. Subsequent actions to resolve differences between the House and Senate, which included the consideration of various House amendments to that Senate amendment, were unsuccessful prior to the beginning of the fiscal year. No other interim CRs that broadly covered the previous fiscal year's projects and activities received congressional action at that time.[2]

---

[1] For further information with regard to CRs, see CRS Report R42647, *Continuing Resolutions: Overview of Components and Recent Practices*, by Jessica Tollestrup.

[2] A narrow automatic continuing resolution, P.L. 113-39, was enacted on September 30 to cover FY2014 pay and allowances for (1) certain members of the Armed Forces, (2) certain Department of Defense (DOD) civilian personnel, and (3) other specified DOD and Department of Homeland Security contractors, during any potential funding gap that might ensue beginning on October 1 (H.R. 3210; P.L. 113-39, 113th Congress). For further information on P.L. 113-39, see CRS Report R41948, *Automatic Continuing Resolutions: Background and Overview of Recent Proposals*, by Jessica Tollestrup.

Because none of the 12 regular appropriations bills for FY2014 were enacted prior to the beginning of the fiscal year, a funding gap commenced on October 1, 2013.[3] Congressional action on FY2014 appropriations between October 2 and October 15 was generally limited to a number of narrow CRs to provide funding for certain programs or classes of individuals.[4]

On October 16, 2013, the Senate passed H.R. 2775 with an amendment that, in part, provided interim continuing appropriations for the previous fiscal year's projects and activities. Later that same day, the House agreed to the Senate amendment to H.R. 2775. The CR (The Continuing Appropriations Act, 2014) was signed into law on October 17, 2013 (P.L. 113-46), thus terminating the funding gap that same day. The act continues FY2013 appropriations (post-sequestration) for the CJS agencies and bureaus until January 15, 2014, or whenever the FY2014 CJS appropriations bill is signed into law.

FY2013 Appropriations

On March 26, 2013, President Obama signed into law the Consolidated and Further Continuing Appropriations Act, 2013 (P.L. 113-6, hereinafter "Consolidated and Further Continuing Appropriations Act").[5] The act provides a total of $60.638 billion for CJS. This amount includes $7.726 billion for the Department of Commerce, $27.305 billion for the Department of Justice, $24.737 billion for the science agencies, and $870.1 million for the related agencies.

Section 3001 of the act provided for a series of rescissions of FY2013 budget authority. Discretionary non-security (as defined at 2 U.S.C. §900(c)(4)(A)) accounts were subject to a 1.877% rescission while discretionary security (as defined at 2 U.S.C. §900(c)(4)(B)) accounts were subject to a 0.1% rescission. Most accounts in the CJS appropriations act were subject to the 1.877% rescission. Only the Foreign Claims Settlement Commission and the International Trade Commission accounts were subject to the 0.1% rescission. Also, per Section 3001, rescissions were applied proportionately to each discretionary account and each item of budget authority and each program, project, or activity (PPA) within each account or item of budget authority (with PPAs being delineated in the act or the explanatory statement published in the March 11 edition of the *Congressional Record*).[6]

Section 3004 of the act is intended to eliminate any amount by which the new budget authority provided in the act exceeds the FY2013 discretionary spending limits in Section 251(c)(2) of the Balanced Budget and Emergency Deficit Control Act, as amended by the Budget Control Act of 2011 and the American Taxpayer Relief Act of 2012. As enacted, this section provides two separate across-the-board rescissions—one for non-security budget authority and one for security

---

[3] A funding gap is the interval during the fiscal year when appropriations for a particular project or activity are not enacted into law, either in the form of a regular appropriations act or a CR. For further information, see CRS Report RS20348, *Federal Funding Gaps: A Brief Overview*, by Jessica Tollestrup.

[4] These CRs include H.J.Res. 70, H.J.Res. 71, H.J.Res. 72, H.J.Res. 73, H.J.Res. 75, H.J.Res. 76, H.J.Res. 77, H.J.Res. 79, H.J.Res. 80, H.J.Res. 82, H.J.Res. 83, H.J.Res. 84, H.J.Res. 85, H.J.Res. 89, H.J.Res. 90, H.J.Res. 91, and H.R. 3230. Of these, only the Department of Defense Survivor Benefits Continuing Appropriations Resolution of 2014 (H.J.Res. 91; P.L. 113-44) was enacted into law.

[5] For more information on the FY2013 appropriations see CRS Report R42440, *Commerce, Justice, Science, and Related Agencies: FY2013 Appropriations*, coordinated by Nathan James, Jennifer D. Williams, and John F. Sargent Jr.

[6] Senator Barbara Mikulski, "Consolidated and Further Continuing Appropriations Act," *Congressional Record*, daily edition, vol. 159, part 34 (March 11, 2013), pp. S1287-S1587.

---

budget authority—of 0%, to be applied at the program, project, and activity level. The section requires the percentages to be increased if the Office of Management and Budget (OMB) estimates that additional rescissions are needed to avoid exceeding the limits. Subsequent to the enactment of P.L. 113-6, OMB calculated that additional rescissions of 0.032% of security budget authority, and 0.2% of non-security budget authority, would be required. Only the Foreign Claims Settlement Commission and the International Trade Commission accounts were subject to the 0.032% rescission. The appropriations provided by the Consolidated and Further Continuing Appropriations Act for each CJS account do not reflect any reductions that resulted from the sequestration ordered by President Obama on March 1, 2013, pursuant to the Budget Control Act of 2011 (P.L. 112-25). (See text box below.)

The Disaster Relief Appropriations Act, 2013 (P.L. 113-2, hereinafter "the Disaster Relief Appropriations Act"), included a total of $363.3 million in supplemental appropriations for CJS agencies. Of the $363.3 million appropriated pursuant to the act, $326.0 million was for the National Oceanic and Atmospheric Administration; $10.0 million was for the Federal Bureau of Investigation; $1.0 million was for the Drug Enforcement Administration; $230,000 was for the Bureau of Alcohol, Tobacco, Firearms, and Explosives; $10.0 million was for the Bureau of Prisons; $15.0 million was for the National Aeronautics and Space Administration; and $1.0 million was for the Legal Services Corporation. The FY2013-enancted amounts presented in the tables below reflect these supplemental appropriations.

The amounts in this report reflect only new appropriations. Therefore, the amounts do not include any rescissions of unobligated or de-obligated balances that may be counted as offsets to newly enacted appropriations, nor do they include any scorekeeping adjustments, such as the balance on the Crime Victims Fund.

Table 1 shows the FY2013-enated appropriations (before sequestration), the Administration's FY2014 request, and the House and Senate Appropriations Committees' recommended amounts, for the Department of Commerce, the Department of Justice, the science agencies, and the related agencies. **Table 14** shows enacted appropriations for these agencies, in detail, for FY2009 through FY2013 (the FY2013 amounts shown in **Table 14** do not reflect sequestration).

A Note on Sequestration

FY2013 discretionary appropriations were considered in the context of the Budget Control Act of 2011 (BCA, P.L. 112-25), which established discretionary spending limits for FY2012-FY2021. The BCA also tasked a Joint Select Committee on Deficit Reduction to develop a federal deficit reduction plan for Congress and the President to enact by January 15, 2012. Because deficit reduction legislation was not enacted by that date, an automatic spending reduction process established by the BCA was triggered; this process consists of a combination of sequestration and lower discretionary spending caps, initially scheduled to begin on January 2, 2013. The "joint committee" sequestration process for FY2013 requires the Office of Management and Budget (OMB) to implement across-the-board spending cuts at the account and program level to achieve equal budget reductions from both defense and nondefense funding at a percentage to be determined, under terms specified in the Balanced Budget and Emergency Deficit Control Act of 1985 (BBEDCA, Title II of P.L. 99-177, 2 U.S.C. 900-922), as amended by the BCA. For further information on the Budget Control Act, see CRS Report R41965, *The Budget Control Act of 2011*, by Bill Heniff Jr., Elizabeth Rybicki, and Shannon M. Mahan.

The American Taxpayer Relief Act (ATRA, P.L. 112-240), enacted on January 2, 2013, made a number of significant changes to the procedures in the BCA that will take place during FY2013. First, the date for the joint committee sequester to be implemented was delayed for two months, until March 1, 2013. Second, the dollar amount of the joint committee sequester was reduced by $24 billion. Third, the statutory caps on discretionary spending for FY2013 (and FY2014) were lowered. For further information on the changes to BCA procedures made by ATRA, see CRS Report R42949, *The American Taxpayer Relief Act of 2012: Modifications to the Budget Enforcement Procedures in the Budget Control Act*, by Bill Heniff Jr.

Pursuant to the BCA, as amended by ATRA, President Obama ordered that the joint committee sequester be implemented on March 1, 2013.[7] The accompanying OMB report indicated a dollar amount of budget authority to be canceled to each account containing non-exempt funds.[8] The sequester will ultimately be applied at the program, project, and activity (PPA) level within each account.[9] Because the sequester was implemented at the time that a temporary continuing resolution was in force, the reductions were calculated on an annualized basis and will be apportioned throughout the remainder of the fiscal year.[10] Although full year FY2013 funding has been enacted, the effect of these reductions on the budgetary resources that will ultimately be available to an agency at either the account or PPA level remains unclear until further guidance is provided by OMB as to how these reductions should be applied.

---

[7] White House, President Obama, Sequestration Order for Fiscal Year 2013 Pursuant to Section 251A of the Balanced Budget and Emergency Deficit Control Act, As Amended, March 1, 2013, available at http://www.whitehouse.gov/sites/default/files/2013sequestration-order-rel.pdf.

[8] Executive Office of the President, Office of Management and Budget, *OMB Report to the Congress on the Joint Committee Sequestration for Fiscal Year 2013*, March 1, 2013, available at http://www.whitehouse.gov/sites/default/files/omb/assets/legislative_reports/fy13ombjcsequestrationreport.pdf.

[9] Ibid., pp. 11, 13.

[10] Ibid, p. 5. For general information on continuing resolutions, see CRS Report R42647, *Continuing Resolutions: Overview of Components and Recent Practices*, by Jessica Tollestrup.

Table 1. CJS Appropriations, FY2013-Enacted (Before Sequestration), FY2014-Requested, and House and Senate Committee-Reported

Budget authority in millions of dollars

Departments and Related Agencies	FY2013 Enacted (Before Sequestration)	FY2014 Request	FY2014 House Committee Reported	FY2014 Senate Committee Reported	FY2014 Enacted
Department of Commerce	$8,069.8a	$8,593.6	$7,543.7	$8,679.0	
Department of Justice	27,326.1b	28,430.5	26,657.5	28,502.7	
Science Agencies	24,752.2c	25,346.8	23,598.9	25,441.8	
Related Agencies	871.0d	962.1	800.5	962.1	
Total	**61,019.2e**	**63,333.1f**	**58,600.6g**	**63,585.7h**	

Source: FY2013-enacted (before sequestration) and FY2014-requested amounts were taken from S.Rept. 113-78. The FY2013-enacted amounts include the rescissions specified in Sections 3001 of the Consolidated and Further Continuing Appropriations Act (P.L. 113-6) and the rescissions ordered by OMB pursuant to Section 3004 of the act. The FY2013-enacted amounts also include supplemental appropriations for the CJS departments and agencies included in the Disaster Relief Appropriations Act, 2013 (P.L. 113-2). The House committee-reported amounts were taken from H.Rept. 113-171 and the Senate committee-reported amounts were taken from S.Rept. 113-78.

Notes: Amounts may not add to totals due to rounding.

a. This amount includes $326.0 million in supplemental funding for the National Oceanic and Atmospheric Administration.

b. This amount includes $10.0 million in supplemental funding for the Federal Bureau of Investigation; $1.0 million in supplemental funding for the Drug Enforcement Administration; $230,000 in supplemental funding for the Bureau of Alcohol, Tobacco, Firearms, and Explosives; and $10.0 million in supplemental funding for the Bureau of Prisons.

c. This amount includes $15.0 million in supplemental funding for the National Aeronautic and Space Administration.

d. This amount includes $1.0 million in supplemental funding for the Legal Services Corporation.

e. This amount does not include $881.6 million in rescissions of prior year unobligated balances.

f. This amount does not include a proposed $1.067 billion in rescissions of prior year unobligated balances.

g. This amount does not include a proposed $879.6 million in rescissions of prior year unobligated balances.

h. This amount does not include a proposed $1.022 billion in rescissions of prior year unobligated balances.

Survey of Selected Issues

Department of Commerce

Some issues Congress might consider while debating FY2014 funding for the Department of Commerce include the following:

- Whether to accept the Administration's proposed $20.1 million increase for the International Trade Administration (ITA) to support the interagency Trade Enforcement Center for the purpose of strengthening U.S. government capacity to monitor and enforce U.S. trade rights under international agreements and other domestic and international trade enforcement authorities.

- Whether to provide additional funding for ITA to support the Administration's Asia Rebalance and the U.S. strategy toward Sub-Saharan Africa and enable identification of more export opportunities for U.S. companies, more rapid and timely business counseling, and enhanced commercial diplomacy and advocacy support.

- Whether to accept the Administration's proposal for additional ITA funding to support implementation of the SelectUSA program, which was established in 2011 by presidential Executive Order to encourage, facilitate, and accelerate foreign direct investment in the United States to create jobs and spur economic growth.

- The progress of the President's Export Control Reform Initiative under the Bureau of Industry and Security (BIS), including oversight of the rebuilding of the control lists and the transfer of items previously controlled as munitions by the Department of State to BIS.

- Whether to fund two new initiatives (the Investing in Manufacturing Communities Fund and Regional Export Challenge Grants) that would be administered by the Economic Development Administration and would support private sector job creation through regional innovation clusters focusing on the export of manufactured goods and services.

- Whether to fund a new program to assess technologies for sharing radio frequency spectrum under the National Telecommunications and Information Administration.

- The funding level for the Census Bureau as it seeks to complete data collection for the 2012 economic census, disseminate information from the 2012 census of governments, and continue research and testing in preparation for the 2020 decennial census.

- Whether to accept the Administration's request under the National Oceanic and Atmospheric Administration (NOAA) of $1.978 billion for environmental satellite acquisition, which is a significant portion (36.3%) of the request for NOAA.

Department of Justice (DOJ)

Some issues Congress might consider while determining funding levels for DOJ accounts include the following:

- Does the Bureau of Prisons have the resources it needs to continue to safely confine a growing federal inmate population?

- Whether to accept the Administration's proposal to eliminate funding for several grant programs under the State and Local Law Enforcement Assistance account, including the State Criminal Alien Assistance Program (SCAAP), the Matching Grant Program for Bulletproof Vests, and the Paul Coverdell Forensic Sciences program.

- Whether to combine the drug and mental health courts program into a problem solving justice program as proposed by the Administration.

- How to prioritize funding for juvenile justice programs—both the formula grant programs as well as the competitive grants?

- Whether to fund the Administration's request for $150.0 million for a comprehensive school safety program under the Community Oriented Policing Services account.

- Whether to accept the Administration's proposal to set aside 7% of the amount appropriated under the State and Local Law Enforcement Assistance, Juvenile Justice Programs, and Research, Evaluation, and Statistics accounts for tribal criminal justice assistance.

- Whether to accept the Administration's proposal to increase the obligation limit on the Crime Victims Fund in order to provide support to the Vision 21 program.[11]

Science Agencies

Among the issues facing the science agencies that Congress may opt to address in the FY2014 appropriations process are the following:

- Whether the current direction for the U.S. human spaceflight program, established in October 2010 by the National Aeronautics and Space Administration Authorization Act of 2010 (P.L. 111-267), can be implemented successfully in a period of increased budgetary constraint, as well as the potential impact of human spaceflight's funding needs on the availability of funding for other National Aeronautics and Space Administration (NASA) programs, such as science, aeronautics, and education.

- Whether and how to prioritize research initiatives at the National Science Foundation (NSF).

- Whether to continue efforts to double funding at NSF and other targeted accounts as previously proposed by the Administration and authorized by Congress, and if so, at what pace.

- Whether to adopt the Administration's proposed government-wide science, technology, engineering, and mathematics (STEM) education program reorganization and consolidation, including proposed changes at NSF, NASA, and the Department of Commerce.

---

[11] Vision 21 is a strategic planning initiative based on an 18-month national assessment by OVC that assesses current and emerging challenges and opportunities facing the field. The initiative addresses identified needs, including the need for more victim related data, research and program evaluation; legal assistance for crime victims; resources for tribal victims; and other related assistance. Of the $45.0 million requested for Vision 21, $20.0 million will be used to support Tribal Assistance for Victims of Violence and $25.0 million will be used for additional victims' services and initiatives. For more information, see U.S. Department of Justice, Office of Justice Programs, *FY2014 Performance Budget*, http://www.justice.gov/jmd/2014justification/pdf/ojp-justification.pdf.

- Whether to continue to restrict the Office of Science and Technology Policy (OSTP) from engaging in certain activities with China or any Chinese-owned company by prohibiting, with limited exceptions, the use of appropriated funds for such activities.

Related Agencies

Some of the issues Congress might consider while determining the FY2014 funding levels for the related agencies include the following:

- Whether to adopt the Administration proposal to eliminate the Legal Service Corporation's restrictions on class action suits and attorneys' fees.

- Whether to approve increased funding for U.S. Trade Representative to add resources and hire additional staff for the purpose of enhancing overall trade enforcement capabilities and supporting the Interagency Trade Enforcement Center (ITEC) to identify and address unfair trade practices among foreign trading partners.

Department of Commerce[12]

The Department of Commerce (Commerce Department) originated in 1903 with the establishment of the Department of Commerce and Labor.[13] The separate Commerce Department was established on March 4, 1913.[14] The department's responsibilities are numerous and quite varied; its activities center on five basic missions: (1) promoting the development of U.S. business and increasing foreign trade; (2) improving the nation's technological competitiveness; (3) encouraging economic development; (4) fostering environmental stewardship and assessment; and (5) compiling, analyzing, and disseminating statistical information on the U.S. economy and population.

The following agencies within the Commerce Department carry out these missions:

- *International Trade Administration (ITA)* seeks to develop the export potential of U.S. firms and improve the trade performance of U.S. industry;

- *Bureau of Industry and Security (BIS)* enforces U.S. export laws consistent with national security, foreign policy, and short-supply objectives;

- *Economic Development Administration (EDA)* provides grants for economic development projects in economically distressed communities and regions;

- *Minority Business Development Agency (MBDA)* seeks to promote private- and public-sector investment in minority businesses;

---

[12] This section was coordinated by Jennifer D. Williams, Specialist in American National Government, CRS Government and Finance Division.

[13] 32 Stat. 825.

[14] 15 U.S.C. 1501.

- *Economics and Statistics Administration (ESA)*, excluding the Census Bureau, provides (1) information on the state of the economy through preparation, development, and interpretation of economic data and (2) analytical support to department officials in meeting their policy responsibilities;

- *Census Bureau*, a component of ESA, collects, compiles, and publishes a broad range of economic, demographic, and social data;

- *National Telecommunications and Information Administration (NTIA)* advises the President on domestic and international communications policy, manages the federal government's use of the radio frequency spectrum, and performs research in telecommunications sciences;

- *United States Patent and Trademark Office (USPTO)* examines and approves applications for patents for claimed inventions and registration of trademarks;

- *National Institute of Standards and Technology (NIST)* assists industry in developing technology to improve product quality, modernize manufacturing processes, ensure product reliability, and facilitate rapid commercialization of products on the basis of new scientific discoveries; and

- *National Oceanic and Atmospheric Administration (NOAA)* provides scientific, technical, and management expertise to (1) promote safe and efficient marine and air navigation; (2) assess the health of coastal and marine resources; (3) monitor and predict the coastal, ocean, and global environments (including weather forecasting); and (4) protect and manage the nation's coastal resources.

FY2013 and FY2014 Appropriations

Table 2 presents the following funding information for the Department of Commerce as a whole and for each of its agencies or bureaus: the amounts provided in the Consolidated and Further Continuing Appropriations Act, the Administration's FY2014 request, and the amounts recommended by the House and Senate Committees on Appropriations.

Table 2. Funding for the Department of Commerce, FY2013 and FY2014

Budget authority in millions of dollars

Bureau or Agency	FY2013 Enacted (Before Sequestration)	FY2014 Request	FY2014 House Committee Reported	FY2014 Senate Committee Reported	FY2014 Enacted
International Trade Administration	$461.4	$519.8	$441.6	$490.6	
Bureau of Industry and Security	99.7	112.1	94.0	112.1	
Economic Development Administration	220.1	320.9	220.5	276.2	
Minority Business Development Agency	28.1	29.3	27.0	29.3	

Bureau or Agency	FY2013 Enacted (Before Sequestration)	FY2014 Request	FY2014 House Committee Reported	FY2014 Senate Committee Reported	FY2014 Enacted
Economics and Statistics Administration (excluding Census)	98.2	104.0	93.4	104.0	
Census Bureau	905.0	982.5	844.7	972.5	
National Telecommunications and Information Administration	45.0	52.1	42.9	52.1	
U.S. Patent and Trademark Office (USPTO)a	2,872.4	3,071.4	3,024.0	3,024.0	
Offsetting Fee Receipts (USPTO)	-2,872.4	-3,071.4	-3,024.0	-3,024.0	
National Institute of Standards and Technology	807.1	928.3	784.0	947.5	
National Oceanic and Atmospheric Administration	5,320.2b	5,439.7	4,915.5	5,589.7	
Departmental Management	85.0	104.9	80.0	104.9	
Total: Department of Commerce	**8,069.8**	**8,593.6**	**7,543.7**	**8,679.0**	

Source: FY2013-enacted (before sequestration) and FY2014-requested amounts were taken from S.Rept. 113-78. The FY2013-enacted amounts include the rescissions specified in Sections 3001 of the Consolidated and Further Continuing Appropriations Act (P.L. 113-6) and the rescissions ordered by OMB pursuant to Section 3004 of the act. The FY2013-enacted amounts also include supplemental appropriations for the CJS departments and agencies included in the Disaster Relief Appropriations Act, 2013 (P.L. 113-2). The House committee-reported amounts were taken from H.Rept. 113-171 and the Senate committee-reported amounts were taken from S.Rept. 113-78.

Notes: Amounts may not add to totals due to rounding.

a. The U.S. Patent and Trademark Office (USPTO) is fully funded by user fees. The fees collected but not obligated during the current year are available for obligation in the following fiscal year and do not count toward the appropriation totals. Only newly appropriated funds count toward the annual appropriation totals. Total figures for the Department of Commerce exclude the USPTO.

b. This amount includes a $326.0 million in supplemental funding for the National Oceanic and Atmospheric Administration.

International Trade Administration (ITA)[15]

The International Trade Administration (ITA) provides export promotion services, works to ensure compliance with trade agreements, administers trade remedies such as antidumping and countervailing duties, and provides analytical support for ongoing trade negotiations. ITA's mission is to improve U.S. prosperity by strengthening the competitiveness of U.S. industry,

---

[15] This section was written by M. Angeles Villarreal, Specialist in International Trade and Finance, CRS Foreign Affairs, Defense, and Trade Division.

promoting trade and investment, and ensuring compliance with trade laws and agreements. ITA strives to accomplish this through the following organizational units: (1) the Manufacturing and Services Unit, which is responsible for certain industry analysis functions and promoting the competitiveness and expansion of the U.S. manufacturing sector; (2) the Market Access and Compliance Unit, which is responsible for monitoring foreign country compliance with trade agreements, identifying compliance problems and market access obstacles, and informing U.S. firms of foreign business practices and opportunities; (3) the Import Administration Unit, which is responsible for administering the trade remedy laws of the United States; (4) the Trade Promotion/U.S. Foreign Commercial Service program, which is responsible for conducting trade promotion programs, providing U.S. companies with export assistance services, and leading interagency advocacy efforts for major overseas projects; and (5) the Executive and Administrative Directorate, which is responsible for providing policy leadership, information technology support, and administration services for all of ITA.

The Consolidated and Further Continuing Appropriations Act provided $461.4 million for ITA in direct appropriations. It anticipated the collection of $11.4 million in user fees, which would raise total FY2013 resources for ITA to $472.8 million. The Administration requests $519.8 million for ITA for FY2014 and anticipates the collection of $9.4 million in user fees, which would raise available funds to $529.2 million. The House committee-reported bill would provide $441.6 million in direct appropriations for this account. The Senate Committee on Appropriations recommends $490.6 million for ITA in direct appropriations.

Bureau of Industry and Security (BIS)[16]

The Bureau of Industry and Security (BIS) administers export controls on dual-use goods and technology through its licensing and enforcement functions. It cooperates with other nations on export control policy and provides assistance to the U.S. business community to comply with U.S. and multilateral export controls. BIS also administers U.S. anti-boycott statutes and is charged with monitoring the U.S. defense industrial base. Authorization for the activities of BIS, the Export Administration Act (50 U.S.C. App. 2401, *et seq.*), last expired in August 2001. On August 17, 2001, President George W. Bush invoked the authorities granted by the International Economic Emergency Powers Act (50 U.S.C. 1703(b)) to continue in effect the system of controls contained in the act and in the Export Administration Regulations (15 C.F.R., Parts 730-799), and these authorities have been renewed yearly. P.L. 113-6 provided $101.8 million ($99.7 million after rescissions) for BIS. The President proposes $112.1 million in FY2014 for BIS. The House Committee on Appropriations recommends $94.0 million, and the Senate Committee on Appropriations recommends the President's full proposal of $112.1 million.

Economic Development Administration (EDA)[17]

The Economic Development Administration (EDA) was created pursuant to the enactment of the Public Works and Economic Development Act of 1965,[18] with the objective of fostering growth

---

[16] This section was written by Ian F. Fergusson, Specialist in International Trade and Finance, CRS Foreign Affairs, Defense, and Trade Division.

[17] This section was written by Eugene Boyd, Analyst in Federalism and Economic Development Policy, CRS Government and Finance Division.

[18] P.L. 89-136; 42 U.S.C. 3121.

in economically distressed areas characterized by high levels of unemployment and low per-capita income levels. Federally designated disaster areas and areas affected by military base realignment or closure (BRAC) are also eligible for EDA assistance. EDA provides grants for public works, economic adjustment in case of natural disasters or mass layoffs, technical assistance, planning, and research.[19]

The Administration's FY2014 budget request proposes to reduce what is EDA's most highly funded program, public works grants. The proposed budget would place greater emphasis on projects intended to support job creation through regional innovation clusters, including those that would support the export of manufactured goods and services. For FY2014, the Administration is requesting $320.9 million, including $282.0 million for EDA programs and activities and $38.9 million for salaries and expenses. P.L. 113-6 appropriated $220.1 million in total funding for EDA, including $183.4 million in support of EDA program and activities and $36.7 million for salaries and expenses. The specific programs and their requested funding levels for FY2014 include

- $40.5 million for the Public Works Program;

- $66.0 million for the Economic Adjustment Assistance Program;

- $27.0 million for the Partnership Planning Grants Program (the proposed successor to the EDA Planning Program);

- $12.0 million for Technical Assistance;

- $1.5 million for Research and Evaluation; and

- $10.0 million for Trade Adjustment Assistance.

The Administration is also requesting funding for two new initiatives that would be administered by EDA:

- $113.0 million for the new Investing in Manufacturing Communities Fund; and

- $12.0 million for the new Regional Export Challenge Grants.

The Administration describes both programs as being consistent with the creation of regional innovation strategies authorized under 42 U.S.C. Section 3722 of the America COMPETES Act (P.L. 111-358).

Table 3. Funding for EDA Programs and Salaries and Expenses, FY2013 and FY2014

Budget authority in millions of dollars

	FY2013 Enacted (Before Sequestration)	FY2014 Request	FY2014 House Committee Reported	FY2014 Senate Committee Reported	FY2014 Enacted
Economic Development Assistance Programs	$183.4	$282.0	$184.5	$237.3	

---

[19] For additional information on EDA's statutory history, see CRS Report R41241, *Economic Development Administration: A Review of Elements of Its Statutory History*, by Eugene Boyd.

	FY2013 Enacted (Before Sequestration)	FY2014 Request	FY2014 House Committee Reported	FY2014 Senate Committee Reported	FY2014 Enacted
Public Works	(77.4)	(40.5)	(95.0)	(100.3)	
Economic Adjustment Assistance	(49.0)	(66.0)	(32.0)	(55.7)	
Planning Grants	(28.4)	(27.0)	(29.0)	(27.0)	
Technical Assistance	(11.8)	(12.0)	(12.0)	(12.0)	
Research and Evaluation	(1.5)	(1.5)	(1.5)	(1.5)	
Trade Adjustment Assistance	(15.5)	(10.0)	(10.0)	(15.8)	
Manufacturing Communities Fund	—	(113.0)	—	—	
Regional Export Challenge	—	(12.0)	—	—	
Innovative Manufacturing Loans	—	—	(5.0)	—	
Regional Innovation Program	—	—	—	(25.0)	
Salaries and Expenses	36.7	38.9	36.0	38.9	
Total	**220.1**	**320.9**	**220.5**	**276.2**	

Source: FY2013-enacted (before sequestration) and FY2014-requested amounts were taken from S.Rept. 113-78. The FY2013-enacted amounts include the rescissions specified in Sections 3001 of the Consolidated and Further Continuing Appropriations Act (P.L. 113-6) and the rescissions ordered by OMB pursuant to Section 3004 of the act. The FY2013-enacted amounts also include supplemental appropriations for the CJS departments and agencies included in the Disaster Relief Appropriations Act, 2013 (P.L. 113-2). The House committee-reported amounts were taken from H.Rept. 113-171 and the Senate committee-reported amounts were taken from S.Rept. 113-78.

Note: Amounts may not add to totals due to rounding.

The Consolidated and Further Continuing Appropriations Act included $220.1 million for EDA programs and agency salaries and expenses. H.R. 2787, as reported by the House Committee on Appropriations, recommends $220.5 million in total appropriations for EDA, including salaries and expenses. A Senate measure, S. 1329, as reported by the Senate Committee on Appropriations, recommends $276.2 million in total funding for EDA, including salaries and expenses. The bill reported by the Senate committee is $55.7 million more than recommended by the House committee. The additional funds recommended by the Senate include significantly higher amounts for Economic Adjustment Assistance and Trade Adjustment Assistance grants than recommended by the House committee. In addition, S. 1329 includes $25.0 million for EDA's Regional Innovation Program (RIP), which awards grants and loan guarantees as authorized under the America COMPETES Reauthorization Act of 2010. RIP supports investments in science parks, regional innovation clusters, and the i6 Challenge program. The accompanying committee report (S.Rept. 113-78) includes language encouraging EDA to consider funding innovative manufacturing and export programs within this amount.

Minority Business Development Agency (MBDA)[20]

The Minority Business Development Agency (MBDA), established by Executive Order 11625 on October 13, 1971, is charged with the lead role in coordinating all of the federal government's minority business programs.[21] As part of its strategic plan, MBDA seeks to develop an industry-focused, data-driven, technical assistance approach to give minority business owners the tools essential for becoming first- or second-tier suppliers to private corporations and the federal government in the new procurement environment. Progress is measured in increased gross receipts, number of employees, and size and scale of firms associated with minority business enterprise. The Consolidated and Further Continuing Appropriations Act provided $28.1 million for the MBDA account. For FY2014, the Administration is requesting $29.3 million in support of MBDA. According to the budget justification document, the proposed MBDA funding level would assist in the creation of 5,000 new jobs and $2 billion in contracts and financing. The House Committee on Appropriations recommends $27.0 million for MBDA funding, while the Senate Committee on Appropriations recommends $29.3 million for MBDA activities.

Economics and Statistics Administration (ESA)[22]

The Economics and Statistics Administration (ESA) provides economic data, analysis, and forecasts to government agencies and, when appropriate, to the public. ESA includes the Census Bureau (discussed separately) and the Bureau of Economic Analysis (BEA). ESA has three core missions: to maintain a system of economic data, to interpret and communicate information about the forces at work in the economy, and to support the information and analytical needs of the executive branch. Funding for ESA includes two primary accounts: ESA headquarters and BEA. ESA headquarters staff provide economic research and policy analysis in support of the Secretary of Commerce, as well as oversight of the Census Bureau and BEA. The BEA account funds BEA activities, among which are producing estimates of national gross domestic product and related measures.

P.L. 113-6 provided $98.2 million for the Economics and Statistics Administration. The Administration's budget request for ESA in FY2014 is $104.0 million. The House Committee on Appropriations recommends $93.4 million, and the Senate Committee on Appropriations recommends the amount requested.

Census Bureau[23]

The U.S. Constitution requires a population census every 10 years, to serve as the basis for apportioning seats in the House of Representatives.[24] Decennial census data also are used for within-state redistricting and in certain formulas that determine the annual distribution of more

---

[20] This section was written by Eugene Boyd, Analyst in Federalism and Economic Development Policy, CRS Government and Finance Division.

[21] 36 *Federal Register* 19967; 3 C.F.R., 1971-1975 Comp. 9. 616.

[22] This section was written by Jennifer D. Williams, Specialist in American National Government, CRS Government and Finance Division.

[23] This section was written by Jennifer D. Williams, Specialist in American National Government, CRS Government and Finance Division.

[24] See Article 1, Section 2, clause 3, as modified by Section 2 of the 14th Amendment.

---

than $450 billion in federal funds to states and localities. The Census Bureau, established as a permanent office on March 6, 1902,[25] conducts the decennial census under Title 13 of the *U.S. Code*, which also authorizes the bureau to collect and compile a wide variety of other demographic, economic, housing, and governmental data.

P.L. 113-6 provided $905.0 million for the Census Bureau, including $250.9 million in the salaries and expenses account and $654.1 million in the periodic censuses and programs account.[26]

In FY2014, the bureau expects, among other activities, to complete data collection for the 2012 economic census, disseminate information from the 2012 census of governments, and continue research and testing in preparation for the 2020 decennial census.

The Administration's FY2014 budget request for the bureau is $982.5 million. Of this amount, $256.0 million is for salaries and expenses, and $726.4 million is for periodic censuses and programs.

The House Committee on Appropriations recommends $844.7 million for the Bureau in FY2014, with $238.9 million for salaries and expenses and $605.9 million for periodic programs. Of the $605.9 million, $390.9 million is to be used for 2020 census preparation. In the view of the ranking Members of the committee and the Subcommittee on Commerce, Justice, Science, and Related Agencies, this amount, "a reduction of $95.7 million (20%) below the request, ... threatens research efforts that would allow the 2020 Census to be conducted at a lower cost."[27]

The Senate Committee on Appropriations' FY2014 recommendation for the Bureau is $972.5 million, of which $256.0 million is for salaries and expenses and $716.4 million is for periodic censuses and programs.[28] The committee "directs the Bureau to continue to use the [working capital fund] only as a repository for reimbursable funds from other agencies and to obligate and execute that funding expeditiously."[29] The committee further directs the Bureau to provide, no later than 120 days after enactment of the act, an updated report on "efforts to evaluate" American Community Survey (ACS) questions "and the steps being taken by the ombudsman position"

---

[25] 32 Stat. 51.

[26] U.S. Congress, Senate Committee on Appropriations, *Departments of Commerce and Justice, and Science, and Related Agencies Appropriations Bill, 2014*, report to accompany S. 1329, 113th Cong., 1st sess., S.Rept. 113-78 (Washington, DC: GPO, 2013), pp. 144-145. The FY2013 amount cited in the Senate committee report for periodic programs includes $18.0 million in unobligated balances, from the Bureau's working capital fund, carried forward as current year budget authority.

[27] U.S. Congress, House Committee on Appropriations, *Commerce, Justice, Science, and Related Agencies Appropriations Bill, 2014*, report to accompany H.R. 2787, 113th Cong., 1st sess., H.Rept. 113-171 (Washington, DC: GPO, 2013), p. 121.

[28] Under S. 1329, the Senate Committee on Appropriations recommends that $10.0 million in unobligated balances from the Census Bureau's working capital fund be available for the Bureau's periodic censuses and programs account. The unobligated balances made available would be in addition to the $716.4 million that would be appropriated for the account from the general fund.

[29] U.S. Congress, Senate Committee on Appropriations, *Departments of Commerce and Justice, and Science, and Related Agencies Appropriations Bill, 2014*, report to accompany S. 1329, 113th Cong., 1st sess., S.Rept. 113-78 (Washington, DC: GPO, 2013), p. 16. For an explanation and critique of the WCF, see U.S. Government Accountability Office, *Intragovernmental Revolving Funds: Commerce Departmental and Census Working Capital Funds Should Better Reflect Key Operating Principles*, GAO-12-56, November 2011.

---

established by the Bureau in FY2013 "to ensure that the ACS is conducted as efficiently and unobtrusively as possible."[30]

H.R. 2787 and S. 1329 contain identical language providing that $1.0 million of the Census Bureau's appropriation "shall be transferred to the 'Office of Inspector General' account for activities associated with carrying out investigations and audits related to the Bureau.... "

National Telecommunications and Information Administration (NTIA)[31]

The National Telecommunications and Information Administration (NTIA) is the executive branch's principal advisory office on domestic and international telecommunications and information technology policies. Its mandate is to provide greater access for all Americans to telecommunications services, support U.S. attempts to open foreign markets, advise on international telecommunications negotiations, and fund grants for new technologies and their applications. Its role in federal spectrum management includes acting as a facilitator and mediator in negotiations among the various federal agencies regarding usage, priority access, causes of interference, and other radio spectrum questions. In recent years, one of the responsibilities of the NTIA has been to oversee the transfer of some radio frequencies from the federal domain to the commercial domain. Many of these frequencies have subsequently been auctioned to the commercial sector and the proceeds paid into the U.S. Treasury.

The NTIA administers some grant programs created by Congress, including the Broadband Technology Opportunities Program (BTOP).[32] BTOP grant programs are in the final stages of completion. The NTIA is commencing a $135 million grant program to help states plan for participation in a new, nationwide public safety broadband network, as required by the Middle Class Tax Relief and Job Creation Act of 2012 (P.L. 112-96). To deploy the new network, the act established the First Responder Network Authority, or FirstNet, as an independent agency within the NTIA and assigned the agency various responsibilities to support FirstNet. FirstNet is funded through the Public Safety Trust Fund, established by Congress to receive revenues from auctions of certain spectrum licenses. FirstNet received an advance of nearly $2 billion from the U.S. Treasury against expected proceeds of sales of spectrum licenses. Another $5 billion in funding is expected from the Public Safety Trust Fund as auction revenues are deposited in the account. The NTIA will also be responsible for collecting auction proceeds and making distributions from the Public Safety Trust Fund until the authorization expires at the end of FY2022.

Grants under the BTOP program included seven projects to develop broadband communications for public safety.[33] After the passage of the Spectrum Act, the NTIA partly suspended funding to

---

[30] U.S. Congress, Senate Committee on Appropriations, *Departments of Commerce and Justice, and Science, and Related Agencies Appropriations Bill, 2014*, report to accompany S. 1329, 113th Cong., 1st sess., S.Rept. 113-78 (Washington, DC: GPO, 2013), pp. 16-17. For a discussion of the ACS, see CRS Report R41532, *The American Community Survey: Development, Implementation, and Issues for Congress*, by Jennifer D. Williams.

[31] This section was written by Linda K. Moore, Specialist in Telecommunications and Spectrum Policy, CRS Resources, Science, and Industry Division.

[32] For a discussion of BTOP grants, see CRS Report R41775, *Background and Issues for Congressional Oversight of ARRA Broadband Awards*, by Lennard G. Kruger.

[33] Locations are Adams County, CO; Charlotte, NC; state of Mississippi; Los Angeles, CA; San Francisco Bay Area, CA; northern New Jersey; and New Mexico.

these projects in order to allow the FirstNet board of directors time to evaluate how the projects might be coordinated with plans for a nationwide network. Furthermore, FirstNet was assigned the sole, national license for public safety broadband; under the Spectrum Act, separate lease agreements are required for spectrum access. In February 2013, the board agreed to move forward with negotiations on leasing agreements with the seven recipients.[34] BTOP grant funds to individual grantees will be released as each leasing agreement is concluded.

The President's budget request for FY2014 is $52.1 million for salaries and expenses, which includes $7.5 million for a new program to assess technologies for sharing radio frequency spectrum. The program would encompass pilot projects over a period of two years in 10 major metropolitan areas. The FY2014 request for broadband grant program oversight is for $24.7 million, roughly 40% of the total budget request.

The House Committee on Appropriations recommends an appropriation of $42.9 million for FY2014, with a requirement that the NTIA provide periodic reports on the status of the seven BTOP grants intended for public safety broadband networks. This amount is $9.2 million less than the President's request.

The Senate Committee on Appropriations recommends an appropriation of $52.1 million, the amount requested by the President.

U.S. Patent and Trademark Office (USPTO)[35]

The U.S. Patent and Trademark Office (USPTO) examines and approves applications for patents on claimed inventions and administers the registration of trademarks. It also helps other federal departments and agencies protect American intellectual property in the international marketplace. The USPTO is funded by user fees paid by customers that are designated as "offsetting collections" and subject to spending limits established by Congress.

For FY2013, P.L. 113-6 provided the USPTO with the budget authority to spend $2.872 billion in fees collected after the two rescissions contained in the bill.

The President's FY2014 budget request includes $3.071 billion in budget authority for the USPTO, the full amount of fees expected to be collected (as determined by the Administration). All fees collected by the USPTO are to be used only for the USPTO as per P.L. 112-29.

Both the House Committee on Appropriations report to accompany H.R. 2787 and the Senate Committee on Appropriations report to accompany S. 1329 recommend providing the USPTO with the budget authority to spend $3.024 billion, the "full amount of fiscal year 2014 fee collections estimated by the Congressional Budget Office." This amount is 1.5% below the figure in the President's request.

---

[34] NTIA Press Release, "FirstNet Board Director Sue Swenson Provides Update on Status of BTOP Negotiations," March 28, 2013, at http://www.ntia.doc.gov/press-release/2013/firstnet-board-member-sue-swenson-provides-update-status-btop-negotiations-0.

[35] This section was written by Wendy H. Schacht, Specialist in Science and Technology Policy, CRS Resources, Science, and Industry Division.

National Institute of Standards and Technology (NIST)[36]

The National Institute of Standards and Technology (NIST) is a laboratory of the Department of Commerce with a mandate to increase the competitiveness of U.S. companies through appropriate support for industrial development of pre-competitive, generic technologies and the diffusion of government-developed technological advances to users in all segments of the American economy. NIST research also provides the measurement, calibration, and quality assurance techniques that underpin U.S. commerce, technological progress, improved product reliability, manufacturing processes, and public safety.

P.L. 113-6 appropriated $807.1 million in FY2013 funding for NIST after accounting for the two rescissions included in the act. Of this amount, $599.5 million is for in-house research under the Scientific and Technical Research and Services (STRS) account, $125.8 million funds the Manufacturing Extension Partnership (MEP) program, $14.2 million is for the Advanced Manufacturing Technology Consortia (AMTech), and $58.8 million supports construction.

The President's FY2014 budget request would provide $928.3 million for NIST. Included in this figure is $693.7 million for the STRS account, $153.1 million for the MEP program, $21.4 million for AMTech, and $60.0 million for construction.

In addition to the appropriations included in the budget proposal that are to be addressed through the annual appropriations process, the Administration includes two new programs that are to be funded through mandatory appropriations (spending that is typically "provided in permanent or multi-year appropriations contained in the authorizing law, and therefore, the funding becomes available automatically each year, without legislative action by Congress"). According to the budget request, NIST will receive $100 million generated by the proceeds of the spectrum auction to "conduct public safety R&D" as part of the Wireless Innovation (WIN) Fund (under provisions of the Middle Class Tax Relief and Job Creation Act of 2012). In addition, the President proposes $1.000 billion in support for the establishment of a National Network for Manufacturing Innovation.

The House Committee on Appropriations report to accompany H.R. 2787 recommends funding NIST at $784.0 million, 15.5% below the budget request. The $609.0 million provided for the STRS account is 12.2% less than the Administration's proposal, while the $120.0 million for MEP is 21.6% below the President's figure. There is no funding provided for AMTech. The $55.0 million for construction is 8.3% less than the budget request.

The Senate Committee on Appropriations report to accompany S. 1329 includes $947.5 million for NIST, 2.1% more than proposed by the President. Funding for the STRS account would amount to $703.0 million, 1.3% higher than the budget request. Support for MEP would total $153.1 million, the same as the Administration's proposal; however, the $31.4 million for AMTech represents a 46.7% increase over the President's recommendation. The $60.0 million for construction is identical to the budget request.

---

[36] This section was written by Wendy H. Schacht, Specialist in Science and Technology Policy, CRS Resources, Science, and Industry Division.

National Oceanic and Atmospheric Administration (NOAA)[37]

The National Oceanic and Atmospheric Administration (NOAA) conducts scientific research in areas such as ecosystems, climate, global climate change, weather, and oceans; supplies information on the oceans and atmosphere; and manages coastal and marine resources. NOAA was created in 1970 by Reorganization Plan No. 4. The reorganization plan was designed to unify a number of the nation's environmental activities and to provide a systematic approach for monitoring, analyzing, and protecting the environment. NOAA's current administrative structure has evolved into five line offices, which include the National Environmental Satellite, Data, and Information Service (NESDIS); the National Marine Fisheries Service (NMFS); the National Ocean Service (NOS); the National Weather Service (NWS); and the Office of Oceanic and Atmospheric Research (OAR). In addition to NOAA's five line offices, Program Support (PS), a cross-cutting budget activity, includes the NOAA Education Program, Corporate Services, Facilities, and the Office of Marine and Aviation Operations (OMAO).

The FY2013-enacted appropriation (before sequestration) for NOAA is $5.320 billion. The Consolidated and Further Continuing Appropriations Act included $4.994 billion for NOAA, and the Disaster Relief Appropriations Act, 2013 (P.L. 113-2) included $326.0 million for NOAA. NOAA's budget is divided into two main accounts, Operations, Research, and Facilities (ORF) and Procurement, Acquisition, and Construction (PAC). P.L. 113-6 included $3.048 billion for ORF, $1.886 billion for PAC, $63.7 million for the Pacific Coastal Salmon Recovery Fund, $342,000 for the Fishermen's Contingency Fund, and negative $4.0 million for the Fisheries Finance Program account. Furthermore, of the $326.0 million provided to NOAA by P.L. 113-2, $140.0 million was included in the ORF account, resulting in a total FY2013 ORF appropriation of $3.188 billion, and $186.0 million was included in the PAC account, resulting in a total FY2013 PAC appropriation of $2.072 billion.

For FY2014, the Administration requests a total of $5.440 billion for NOAA.[38] The Administration proposes funding ORF at $3.278 billion, PAC at $2.118 billion, the Pacific Coastal Salmon Recovery Fund at $50.0 million, the Fishermen's Contingency Fund at $350,000, and the Fisheries Finance Program at negative $6.0 million.[39] The House Committee on Appropriations recommends a total of $4.916 billion for NOAA. The House committee-reported bill would fund ORF at $2.907 billion, PAC at $1.979 billion, the Pacific Coastal Salmon Recovery Fund at $35.0 million, the Fishermen's Contingency Fund at $350,000, and the Fisheries Finance Program at negative $6.0 million. The Senate Committee on Appropriations recommends a total of $5.590 billion for NOAA. The Senate committee-reported bill would fund ORF at $3.296 billion, PAC at $2.084 billion, the Pacific Coastal Salmon Recovery Fund at $65.0 million, the Fishermen's Contingency Fund at $350,000, and the Fisheries Finance Program at negative $6.0 million. The Senate bill would also provide $150.0 million for a new Fisheries Disaster Mitigation Fund. The fund would help alleviate economic impacts associated with commercial fishery failures, fishery resource disasters, and state and federal regulations.

---

[37] This section was written by Harold F. Upton, Analyst in Natural Resources Policy, CRS Resources, Science, and Industry Division.

[38] The NOAA FY2014 total includes requested funding levels for the following accounts, Operations, Research, and Facilities (ORF); Procurement, Acquisition, and Construction (PAC); the Pacific Coastal Salmon Recovery Fund; the Fishermen's Contingency Fund; and the Fisheries Finance Program.

[39] The Fisheries Finance Program Account would provide a negative subsidy estimated at $6.0 million.

The Administration's FY2014 request for NESDIS satellite systems acquisition and construction is $1.978 billion, which is 93.4% of the Administration's request for PAC funding and 36.3% of the total request for NOAA. The Senate Committee on Appropriations recommends $1.945 billion for NESDIS PAC acquisition and construction, while the House Committee on Appropriations recommends $1.857 billion.

Department of Justice (DOJ)[40]

Established by an act of 1870[41] with the Attorney General at its head, DOJ provides counsel for the government in federal cases and protects citizens through law enforcement. It represents the federal government in all proceedings, civil and criminal, before the Supreme Court. In legal matters, generally, the department provides legal advice and opinions, upon request, to the President and executive branch department heads. The major functions of DOJ agencies and offices are described below.

- *United States Attorneys* prosecute criminal offenses against the United States; represent the federal government in civil actions; and initiate proceedings for the collection of fines, penalties, and forfeitures owed to the United States.

- *United States Marshals Service (USMS)* provides security for the federal judiciary, protects witnesses, executes warrants and court orders, manages seized assets, detains and transports unsentenced prisoners, and apprehends fugitives.

- *Federal Bureau of Investigation (FBI)* investigates violations of federal criminal law; helps protect the United States against terrorism and hostile intelligence efforts; provides assistance to other federal, state, and local law enforcement agencies; and shares jurisdiction with Drug Enforcement Administration over federal drug violations.

- *Drug Enforcement Administration (DEA)* investigates federal drug law violations; coordinates its efforts with state, local, and other federal law enforcement agencies; develops and maintains drug intelligence systems; regulates legitimate controlled substances activities; and conducts joint intelligence-gathering activities with foreign governments.

- *Bureau of Alcohol, Tobacco, Firearms and Explosives (ATF)* enforces federal law related to the manufacture, importation, and distribution of alcohol, tobacco, firearms, and explosives. It was transferred from the Department of the Treasury to DOJ by the Homeland Security Act of 2002 (P.L. 107-296).

- *Federal Prison System* (*Bureau of Prisons, BOP*) provides for the custody and care of the federal prison population, the maintenance of prison-related facilities, and the boarding of sentenced federal prisoners incarcerated in state and local institutions.

---

[40] This section was written by Nathan James, Analyst in Crime Policy; Kristin M. Finklea, Specialist in Domestic Security; William J. Krouse, Specialist in Domestic Security and Crime Policy; and Lisa N. Sacco, Analyst in Illicit Drugs and Crime Policy; CRS Domestic Social Policy Division.

[41] 28 U.S.C. §501

- *Office on Violence Against Women (OVW)* coordinates legislative and other initiatives relating to violence against women and administers grant programs to help prevent, detect, and stop violence against women, including domestic violence, sexual assault, and stalking.

- *Office of Justice Programs (OJP)* manages and coordinates the activities of the Bureau of Justice Assistance, Bureau of Justice Statistics, National Institute of Justice, Office of Juvenile Justice and Delinquency Prevention, and the Office of Victims of Crime.

- *Community Oriented Policing Services (COPS)* advances the practice of community policing by awarding grants to law enforcement agencies to hire and train community policing professionals, acquire and deploy crime-fighting technologies, and develop and test innovative policing strategies.

Most crime control has traditionally been a state and local responsibility. With the passage of the Crime Control Act of 1968 (P.L. 90-351), however, the federal role in the administration of criminal justice has increased incrementally. Since 1984, Congress has approved five major omnibus crime control bills, designating new federal crimes, penalties, and additional law enforcement assistance programs for state and local governments.[42]

FY2013 and FY2014 Appropriations

The FY2013-enacted appropriation (before sequestration) for the DOJ is $27.326 billion. This includes $27.305 billion the DOJ received under the Consolidated and Further Continuing Appropriations Act and $21.3 million in supplemental appropriations under the Disaster Relief Appropriations Act. The Administration requests a total of $28.405 billion for DOJ for FY2014 (see **Table 4**). The House committee-reported bill includes a total of $26.658 billion for the DOJ while the Senate committee-reported bill includes $28.503 billion. As shown in **Table 4**, the Senate committee-reported bill includes a higher level of funding for the DOJ's law enforcement agencies (the USMS, FBI, DEA, and ATF), the U.S. Attorneys, and the federal prison system. In addition, the proposed appropriations for DOJ grant programs under the Senate committee-reported bill are greater than the House Committee on Appropriation's proposed level.

Table 4. Funding for the Department of Justice, FY2013 and FY2014

Budget authority in millions of dollars

Accounts	FY2013 Enacted (Before Sequestration)	FY2014 Request	FY2014 House Committee Reported	FY2014 Senate Committee Reported	FY2014 Enacted
General Administration	$528.5	$563.0	$514.3	$567.0	
General Administration	(141.3)	(152.1)	(129.7)	(152.1)	
Administrative Review & Appeals	(303.0)	(329.1)	(303.0)	(329.1)	

---

[42] See, for example, the Crime Control Act of 1984 (P.L. 98-473); the Anti-Drug Abuse Act of 1986 (P.L. 99-570); the Anti-Drug Abuse Act of 1988 (P.L. 100-690); the Crime Control Act of 1990 (P.L. 101-647); and the Violent Crime Control and Law Enforcement Act of 1994 (P.L. 103-322).

Accounts	FY2013 Enacted (Before Sequestration)	FY2014 Request	FY2014 House Committee Reported	FY2014 Senate Committee Reported	FY2014 Enacted
Office of the Inspector General	(84.2)	(85.8)	(81.5)	(85.8)	
U.S. Parole Commission	12.5	13.0	12.0	13.0	
Legal Activities	3,149.9	3,281.9	3,077.1	3,284.2	
General legal activities	(862.7)	(902.6)	(822.2)	(905.6)	
United States Attorneys	(1,928.9)	(2,007.7)	(1,887.0)	(2,007.7)	
Other[a]	(358.3)	(370.9)	(367.9)	(370.9)	
United States Marshals Service	2,794.2	2,849.6	2,684.8	2,857.1	
National Security Division	88.2	96.2	91.8	96.2	
Interagency Law Enforcement	511.0	523.0	486.0	523.0	
Federal Bureau of Investigation	8,104.6[b]	8,442.7	8,121.9	8,472.7	
Drug Enforcement Administration	2,009.4[c]	2,068.0	1,969.6	2,068.0	
Bureau of Alcohol, Tobacco, Firearms and Explosives	1,129.7[d]	1,229.5	1,142.0	1,229.5	
Federal Prison System	6,779.6[e]	6,939.1	6,672.7	6,939.1	
Office on Violence Against Women	407.9	412.5	413.0	417.0	
Office of Justice Programs	1,592.8	1,569.2	1,472.3	1,642.3	
Research, Evaluation, and Statistics	(124.4)	(134.4)	(114.0)	(129.0)	
State and Local Law Enforcement Assistance	(1,116.8)	(1,005.0)	(1,065.0)	(1,137.0)	
Juvenile Justice Programs	(273.7)	(332.5)	(196.0)	(279.0)	
Public Safety Officers Benefits	(78.0)	(97.3)	(97.3)	(97.3)	
Community Oriented Policing Services	217.9	439.5	—	393.5	
Crime Victims Fund (CVF)	730.0	800.0	745.0	765.0	
Offsetting Receipts (CVF)	-730.0	-800.0	-745.0	-765.0	
Total: Department of Justice	**27,326.1**	**28,430.5**	**26,657.5**	**28,502.7**	

Source: FY2013-enacted (before sequestration) and FY2014-requested amounts were taken from S.Rept. 113-78. The FY2013-enacted amounts include the rescissions specified in Sections 3001 of the Consolidated and Further Continuing Appropriations Act (P.L. 113-6) and the rescissions ordered by OMB pursuant to Section 3004 of the act. The FY2013-enacted amounts also include supplemental appropriations for the CJS departments and agencies included in the Disaster Relief Appropriations Act, 2013 (P.L. 113-2). The House committee-reported amounts were taken from H.Rept. 113-171 and the Senate committee-reported amounts were taken from S.Rept. 113-78.

Note: Amounts may not add to totals due to rounding.

a.   "Other" includes accounts for the Antitrust Division, Vaccine Injury Compensation Trust Fund, U.S. Trustee System Fund, Foreign Claims Settlement Commission, Fees and Expenses of Witnesses, Community Relations Service, and the Asset Forfeiture Fund.

b.   This amount includes $10.0 million in supplemental funding for the Federal Bureau of Investigation.

c.   This amount includes $1.0 million in supplemental funding for the Drug Enforcement Administration.

d.   This amount includes $230,000 in supplemental funding for the Bureau of Alcohol, Tobacco, Firearms, and Explosives

e.   This amount includes $10.0 million in supplemental funding for the Bureau of Prisons.

General Administration

The General Administration account provides funds for salaries and expenses for the Attorney General's office, the Inspector General's office, and other programs designed to ensure that the collaborative efforts of DOJ agencies are coordinated to help represent the government and fight crime as efficiently as possible. The Consolidated and Further Continuing Appropriations Act provided nearly $528.5 million for the General Administration account. The Administration's FY2014 request includes $563.0 million for General Administration. The House Committee on Appropriations recommends nearly $514.3 million for this account. The Senate committee-reported bill would provide $567.0 million for General Administration.

General Administration

The General Administration account includes funding for Salaries and Expenses for DOJ administration as well as for Justice Information Sharing Technology. Prior to the National Drug Intelligence Center's (NDIC's) closure, it was funded through the General Administration account. In addition, this account previously funded Law Enforcement Wireless Communications before funding for related activities was shifted to the FBI.

The Consolidated and Further Continuing Appropriations Act provided nearly $141.3 million for General Administration. The Administration's FY2014 request includes almost $152.1 million for these activities. The House committee-reported bill would provide $129.7 million for General Administration. The Senate Committee on Appropriations recommends nearly $152.1 million for this account.

Administrative Review and Appeals (ARA)

Administrative Review and Appeals (ARA) includes the Executive Office of Immigration Review (EOIR) and the Office of the Pardon Attorney (OPA). The Attorney General is responsible for the review and adjudication of immigration cases in coordination with the Department of Homeland Security's (DHS's) efforts to secure the nation's borders. The EOIR handles these matters, and the OPA receives and reviews petitions for executive clemency.

The Consolidated and Further Continuing Appropriations Act provided $303.0 million for Administrative Review and Appeals. The Administration's FY2014 request includes $329.1 million for this account. The House Committee on Appropriations recommends $303.0 million for Administrative Review and Appeals. The Senate committee-reported bill would provide $329.1 million for this account.

Office of the Inspector General (OIG)

The Office of the Inspector General (OIG) is responsible for detecting and deterring waste, fraud, and abuse involving DOJ programs and personnel; promoting economy and efficiency in DOJ operations; and investigating allegations of departmental misconduct. The Consolidated and Further Continuing Appropriations Act provided $84.2 million for the OIG. The Administration's FY2014 request includes $85.8 million for OIG activities. The House Committee on Appropriations recommends $81.5 million for this account. The Senate committee-reported bill would provide $85.8 million for OIG activities.

U.S. Parole Commission

The U.S. Parole Commission adjudicates parole requests for prisoners who are serving felony sentences under federal and District of Columbia code violations. The Parole Commission received a total of $12.5 million under the Consolidated and Further Continuing Appropriations Act. The Administration's FY2014 request for the commission is $13.0 million. The House Committee on Appropriations recommends $12.0 million for the commission for FY2014 while the Senate Committee on Appropriations recommends $13.0 million.

Legal Activities

The Legal Activities account includes several subaccounts: general legal activities, U.S. Attorneys, and other legal activities. The Consolidated and Further Continuing Appropriations Act provided almost $3.150 billion for Legal Activities. The Administration's FY2014 request includes nearly $3.282 billion for this account. The House committee-reported bill would provide $3.077 billion for Legal Activities. The Senate Committee on Appropriations recommends $3.284 billion for this account.

General Legal Activities

The General Legal Activities account funds the Solicitor General's supervision of the department's conduct in proceedings before the Supreme Court. It also funds several departmental divisions (tax, criminal, civil, environment and natural resources, legal counsel, civil rights, INTERPOL, and dispute resolution). The Consolidated and Further Continuing Appropriations Act provided $862.7 million for the General Legal Activities account. The Administration is requesting $902.6 million for this account for FY2014. The House Committee on Appropriations recommends $822.2 million for General Legal Activities. The Senate committee-reported bill would provide $905.6 million for this account.

Office of the U.S. Attorneys

The U.S. Attorneys enforce federal laws through prosecution of criminal cases and represent the federal government in civil actions in all of the 94 federal judicial districts. For FY2013, under P.L. 113-6, Congress appropriated $1.929 billion for the U.S. Attorneys. For FY2014, the

Administration's request includes $2.008 billion. The FY2014 request includes an increase of $26.5 million to address a rise in financial and mortgage fraud cases. While the House-reported bill includes $1.887 billion for the U.S. Attorneys, the Senate-reported bill includes the same amount as requested by the Administration.

Other Legal Activities

Other Legal Activities includes the Antitrust Division, the Vaccine Injury Compensation Trust Fund, the U.S. Trustee System Fund (which is responsible for maintaining the integrity of the U.S. bankruptcy system by, among other things, prosecuting criminal bankruptcy violations), the Foreign Claims Settlement Commission, the Fees and Expenses of Witnesses, the Community Relations Service, and the Assets Forfeiture Fund. The Consolidated and Further Continuing Appropriations Act provided nearly $358.3 million for the Other Legal Activities accounts. The Administration's FY2014 request includes almost $370.9 million for these accounts. The House Committee on Appropriations recommends $367.9 million for Other Legal Activities. The Senate committee-reported bill would provide nearly $370.9 million for these accounts.

U.S. Marshals Service (USMS)

The U.S. Marshals Service (USMS) is responsible for the protection of the federal judicial process, including protecting judges, attorneys, witnesses, and jurors. In addition, the USMS provides physical security in courthouses, safeguards witnesses, transports prisoners from court proceedings, apprehends fugitives, executes warrants and court orders, and seizes forfeited property. Under the Consolidated and Further Continuing Appropriations Act, Congress eliminated funding for the Office of the Federal Detention Trustee account and instead provided funding for a Federal Prisoner Detention account under the USMS. Funding under this account will be used to cover the costs associated with the care of federal detainees.

The Consolidated and Further Continuing Appropriations Act provided a total of $2.794 billion for the USMS, which included $1.171 billion for its Salaries and Expenses (S&E) account, $9.8 million for its Construction account, and $1.613 billion for the Federal Prisoner Detention account. The Administration requests $2.850 billion for the USMS for FY2014, which includes $1.204 billion for the S&E account, $10.0 million for the Construction account, and $1.636 billion for the Federal Prisoner Detention account. The House Committee on Appropriations recommends a total of $2.685 billion for the USMS, which includes $1.155 billion for the S&E account and $1.520 billion for the Federal Prisoner Detention account. The Senate Committee on Appropriations recommends a total of $2.857 billion for the USMS for FY2014, which includes $1.212 billion for the S&E account and $1.636 billion for the Federal Prisoner Detention account.

National Security Division (NSD)

The National Security Division (NSD) coordinates DOJ's national security and terrorism missions through law enforcement investigations and prosecutions. The NSD was established in DOJ in response to the recommendations of the Commission on the Intelligence Capabilities of the United States Regarding Weapons of Mass Destruction (WMD Commission), and authorized by Congress on March 9, 2006, in the USA PATRIOT Improvement and Reauthorization Act of 2005. Under the NSD, the DOJ resources of the Office of Intelligence Policy and Review and the Criminal Division's Counterterrorism and Counterespionage Sections were consolidated to coordinate all intelligence-related resources and to ensure that criminal intelligence information is shared, as appropriate. For FY2013, under P.L. 113-6, Congress appropriated $88.2 million for the NSD. For FY2014, the Administration requests $96.2 million for the NSD. While the House-reported bill would provide $91.8 million, the Senate-reported bill would provide the same amount as requested by the Administration.

Interagency Law Enforcement

The Interagency Law Enforcement account reimburses departmental agencies for their participation in the Organized Crime Drug Enforcement Task Force (OCDETF) program. Organized into nine regional task forces, this program combines the expertise of federal agencies with the efforts of state and local law enforcement to disrupt and dismantle major narcotics-trafficking and money-laundering organizations. From DOJ, the federal agencies that participate in OCDETF are the DEA; the FBI; the ATF; the USMS; the Tax and Criminal Divisions of DOJ; and the U.S. Attorneys. From the Department of Homeland Security, Immigration and Customs Enforcement and the U.S. Coast Guard participate in OCDETF. In addition, from the Department of the Treasury, the Internal Revenue Service and Treasury Office of Enforcement also participate in OCDETF. Moreover, state and local law enforcement agencies participate in approximately 90% of all OCDETF investigations.

The Consolidated and Further Continuing Appropriations Act provided nearly $511.0 million for the Interagency Law Enforcement account. For FY2014, the Administration is requesting $523.0 million for this account. The House Committee on Appropriations recommends $486.0 million for the Interagency Law Enforcement. The Senate committee-reported bill would provide $523.0 million for this account.

Federal Bureau of Investigation (FBI)

The FBI is the lead federal investigative agency charged with defending the country against foreign terrorist and intelligence threats; enforcing federal laws; and providing leadership and criminal justice services to federal, state, municipal, tribal, and territorial law enforcement agencies and partners. Since the September 11, 2001 (9/11), terrorist attacks, the FBI has reorganized and reprioritized its efforts to focus on preventing terrorism and related criminal activities. From FY2001 through FY2012, Congress has more than doubled direct appropriations for the FBI from $3.32 billion to $8.118 billion, or a 144.5% increase.[43] Under P.L. 113-6, for FY2013, Congress appropriated $8.095 billion for the FBI. In addition, Congress appropriated $10.0 million for FY2013 in a supplemental appropriation for disaster relief (P.L. 113-2), bringing the FY2013 total appropriation for the FBI to $8.105 billion.

For FY2014, the Administration's request includes $8.443 billion: this amount includes $8.362 billion for FBI salaries and expenses and $81.0 million for construction. The amount for salaries and expenses includes the following increases:

- $86.6 million for next generation cyber initiative;

---

[43] The FY2010-enacted amount does not reflect a $50 million rescission or a $24 million supplemental appropriation.

- $100.0 million for the National Instant Criminal Background Check System (NICS);

- $7.4 million to support the FBI Biometric Center of Excellence and the Department of Defense Biometrics Fusion Center;

- $6.0 million to improve surveillance requirements; and

- $15.0 million to bolster financial and mortgage fraud crimes.

The requested $100 million increase for NICS anticipates that Congress will pass legislation to require background checks for intrastate, private firearms transfers, as proposed by the President under his gun violence reduction plan.[44] The House-reported bill includes $8.122 billion for the FBI; the Senate-reported bill, $8.473 billion.

Drug Enforcement Administration (DEA)

The Drug Enforcement Administration (DEA) is the only single-mission federal agency tasked with enforcing the nation's controlled substance laws in order to reduce the availability and abuse of illicit drugs and the diversion of licit drugs for illicit purposes. DEA's enforcement efforts include the disruption and dismantling of drug trafficking and money laundering organizations through drug interdiction and seizures of illicit revenues and assets derived from these organizations. DEA continues to face evolving challenges in limiting the supply of illicit drugs as well as reducing drug trafficking across the Southwest border with Mexico into the United States. DEA plays a key role in the Administration's Southwest Border Initiative to counter drug-related border violence, focusing on the convergent threats of illegal drugs, drug-related violence, and terrorism in the region. DEA also has an active role in the Administration's Prescription Drug Abuse Prevention Plan, targeting improper prescribing practices and promoting proper disposal of unused prescription drugs.

The FY2013-enacted appropriation for the DEA, before sequestration, is approximately $2.009 billion, which includes a $1.0 million supplemental appropriation. For FY2014, the Administration requests $2.068 billion for the DEA. The House committee-reported bill would provide $1.970 billion for this account, and the Senate Committee on Appropriations recommends $2.068 billion for the DEA account.

Bureau of Alcohol, Tobacco, Firearms, and Explosives (ATF)

The ATF enforces federal criminal law related to the manufacture, importation, and distribution of alcohol, tobacco, firearms, and explosives. ATF works independently and through partnerships with industry groups; international, state, and local governments; and other federal agencies to investigate and reduce crime involving firearms and explosives, acts of arson, and illegal trafficking of alcohol and tobacco products. From FY2001 through FY2012, Congress has increased the direct appropriation for ATF, from $771.0 million to $1.152 billion, a 49.4% increase. For FY2013, under P.L. 113-6, Congress appropriated $1.129 billion for ATF. Also, for

---

[44] For further information, see CRS Report R42987, *Gun Control Proposals in the 113th Congress: Universal Background Checks, Gun Trafficking, and Military Style Firearms,* by William J. Krouse.

disaster relief, Congress appropriated a supplemental appropriation of $230,000 for ATF (P.L. 113-2), bringing the total FY2013 appropriations for that agency to $1.130 billion.

For FY2014, the Administration's request includes $1.23 billion for ATF. The FY2013 request includes $51.1 million to improve the capabilities of the National Tracing Center (NTC),[45] $22.0 million to upgrade National Integrated Ballistics Information Network (NIBIN).[46] While the House-reported bill would provide ATF with $1.142 billion, the Senate-reported bill would match the Administration's request.

Also, the Administration requests the elimination of two long-standing provisos, in the ATF salaries and expenses appropriations language, that prohibit ATF from:

- altering the regulatory definition of "curios and relics,"[47] and

- requiring federally licensed gun dealers to conduct physical inventories.[48]

Under P.L. 113-6, Congress included futurity language (in the current fiscal year and any fiscal year thereafter) in both of these provisions that appears to be intended to make these provisos permanent law.[49] Neither the House- nor Senate-reported bill addresses either of these provisions. The House-reported bill, however, includes additional "futurity language" (in the current fiscal year and any fiscal year thereafter) in two other standalone provisions, which also appears to be intended to make these provisions permanent law:

---

[45] The NTC is located in Martinsburg, West Virginia. At this site, ATF employees can conduct traces of firearms produced after 1968 by following firearms serial numbers from the first federally licensed firearms manufacturer or importer to the federally licensed gun dealer, who first transferred the firearm in question to an unlicensed person and the ATF Form 4473 maintained by that dealer as required by law to document that transfer.

[46] NIBIN consists of several regional computer networks administered by ATF to allow federal, state, local, and tribal law enforcement to share ballistic images of bullets and cartridge casings recovered at crime scenes. When magnified the distinctive striations made by the rifling of a barrel on a bullet and the markings made by firing pins and ejectors on a cartridge casing can be linked to an individual firearm, much like a fingerprint can be linked to an individual person.

[47] Congress has included this proviso in the ATF salaries and expenses appropriations language, for FY1996 and every year thereafter, in response to an ATF regulatory proposal to amend the definition of "curios or relics," because of concerns about the volume of surplus military firearms—particularly World War II era firearms—that could be potentially imported into the United States. For the definition of "curios or relics," see 27 CFR § 478.11, which generally include firearms that are 50 years old, of museum interest, or derive a substantial amount of their value from the fact that they are novel, rare, bizarre, or because they are associated with some historical figure, period, or event. For a list of "curios and relics," go to http://www.atf.gov/publications/firearms/curios-relics/. Federally licensed firearms collectors are authorized to engage in limited interstate transfers of "curios and relics," whereas in nearly all cases an unlicensed person must engage the services of a federally licensed gun dealer to facilitate interstate firearms transfers to another unlicensed person.

[48] Congress has included this proviso in the ATF salaries and expenses appropriations language, for FY2004 and every year thereafter, which prohibits that agency from using any appropriated funding to require federally licensed gun dealers (otherwise referred to as federal firearms licensees, or FFLs) to conduct inventories prior to an ATF inspection. This provision was originally part of the FY2004 Tiahrt amendment, known for its sponsor in CJS appropriations subcommittee markup, Representative Todd Tiahrt. The Tiahrt amendment included three other provisos that limit ATF's authority to release unexpurgated firearms trace data publically, require that certain caveats about the limitations of trace data be appended to any such public data releases, and requires the FBI to destroy records on approved firearms-related background checks through the National Instant Criminal Background Check be destroyed within 24 hours.

[49] Consolidated and Further Continuing Appropriations Act, 2013 (P.L. 113-6; March 26, 2013; 127 Stat. 198, 248).

- Section 517 would address the export of certain firearms parts and accessories to Canada,[50] and

- Section 518 would address the importation of "curios or relics" firearms, parts, or ammunition.[51]

As in years past, the Senate-reported bill includes similar provisions, but they do not include "futurity language." In response to a controversial Southwest border gun trafficking investigation conducted by ATF, known as Fast and Furious, Section 216 of both bills would prohibit any federal agent from facilitating the transfer of an operable firearm to any individual associated with a drug cartel, unless that firearm were to be continuously monitored or under the federal agent's control at all times.

Federal Prison System (Bureau of Prisons, BOP)

The Bureau of Prisons (BOP) was established in 1930 to house federal inmates, to professionalize the prison service, and to ensure consistent and centralized administration of the federal prison system.[52] The mission of the BOP is to protect society by confining offenders in prisons and community-based facilities that are safe, humane, cost-efficient, and appropriately secure, and that provide work and other self-improvement opportunities for inmates so that they can become productive citizens after they are released.[53] The BOP currently operates 118 correctional facilities across the country.[54] The BOP also contracts with Residential Re-entry Centers (RRCs) (i.e., halfway houses) to provide assistance to inmates nearing release.[55] RRCs provide inmates with a structured and supervised environment along with employment counseling, job placement services, financial management assistance, and other programs and services.[56]

Congress funds the BOP's operations through two accounts under the Federal Prison System heading: Salaries and Expenses (S&E) and Buildings and Facilities (B&F). The S&E account (i.e., the operating budget) provides for the custody and care of federal inmates and for the daily maintenance and operations of correctional facilities, regional offices, and BOP's central office in Washington, DC. It also provides funding for the incarceration of federal inmates in state, local, and private facilities. The B&F account (i.e., the capital budget) provides funding for the construction of new facilities and the modernization, repair, and expansion of existing facilities. In addition to appropriations for the S&E and B&F accounts, Congress usually places a cap on

---

[50] This provision has been included in the CJS appropriations since FY2006. It is a response to regulations promulgated during the Clinton Administration that were based on the Organization of American States (OAS) Model Regulations for the Control of the International Movement of Firearms. These regulations arguably have made it cost prohibitive to export certain firearms parts and accessories to Canada.

[51] This provision has also been included in the CJS appropriations since FY2006. It is designed to prevent the Department of State from denying applications to import certain firearms, parts, or ammunition that were previously provided by the United States as military aid to foreign governments. Examples of such firearms could include World War Two-era, semiautomatic M-1 Carbines and 1911 Colt pistols. ATF has generally opposed the importation of such firearms back into the United States.

[52] U.S. Department of Justice, Bureau of Prisons, *About the Bureau of Prisons*, http://www.bop.gov/about/index.jsp.

[53] U.S. Department of Justice, Bureau of Prisons, *Mission and Vision of the Bureau of Prisons*, http://www.bop.gov/about/mission.jsp.

[54] U.S. Department of Justice, Bureau of Prisons, *About the Bureau of Prisons*, http://www.bop.gov/about/index.jsp.

[55] U.S. Department of Justice, Bureau of Prisons, *Community Corrections*, http://www.bop.gov/locations/cc/index.jsp.

[56] Ibid.

---

the amount of revenue generated by the Federal Prison Industries (FPI)[57] that can be used for administrative expenses in the annual CJS appropriations bill. Although Congress does not appropriate funding for the administrative expenses of FPI, the administrative expenses cap is scored as enacted budget authority.

For FY2013, the BOP received a total of $6.780 billion (before sequestration), which included $6.770 under the Consolidated and Further Continuing Appropriations Act ($6.679 billion for the S&E account and $88.1 million for the B&F account) and $10.0 million under the Disaster Relief Appropriations Act.

The Administration requests $6.939 billion for the BOP for FY2014, of which $6.831 billion is for the S&E account and $105.2 million is for the B&F account. For FY2014 the Administration requests $97.1 million under the BOP's S&E account to staff and open three prisons (Thomson, IL; Hazelton, WV; and Yazoo City, MS) and $43.0 million to expand residential drug treatment, prisoner re-entry, and rehabilitative programs. The House Committee on Appropriations recommends $6.673 billion for the BOP, which includes $6.580 billion for the S&E account and $90.0 million for the B&F account. The Senate Committee on Appropriations recommends a total of $6.939 billion for the BOP, which includes $6.831 billion for the S&E account and $105.2 million for the B&F account. The Senate committee-reported bill would fully fund the Administration's request to staff and open new prisons and expand residential drug treatment, prisoner re-entry, and rehabilitative programs.

A recurring issue is whether the BOP has adequate resources, both in terms of personnel and infrastructure, to properly manage the burgeoning federal prison population.[58] Prison population growth and prison crowding continue to be a major concern for the BOP. The number of inmates held in BOP facilities grew from 125,560 in FY2000 to 177,556 in FY2012.[59] During that same time period, prison crowding grew from 32% over rated capacity to 38% over rated capacity, even though the number of facilities operated by BOP increased from 97 to 118.[60] The BOP estimates that by FY2018 the federal prison system will be operating at 41% over rated capacity.[61] The growing federal prison population has not only resulted in more crowded prisons, but it has also strained the BOP's ability to properly manage and care for federal inmates. The BOP reports that the staff-to-inmate ratio has increased from 3.57 to 1 in FY1997 to 4.84 to 1 in FY2012.[62] As a point of comparison, in FY2009 the five states with the highest prison populations had an average inmate-to-staff ratio of 3.1 to 1.[63] The growing federal prison population has also required the BOP to dedicate more resources to caring (e.g., providing health care, food, and clothing) and providing programming (e.g., substance abuse treatment, educational programming, and work/vocational opportunities) for inmates. In addition, the

---

[57] For more information on FPI, see CRS Report RL32380, *Federal Prison Industries: Overview and Legislative History*, by Nathan James.

[58] For more information on the issues related to the growing federal prison population, see CRS Report R42937, *The Federal Prison Population Buildup: Overview, Policy Changes, Issues, and Options*, by Nathan James.

[59] Data provided to CRS from the U.S. Department of Justice, Bureau of Prisons.

[60] Ibid.

[61] U.S. Department of Justice, Bureau of Prisons, *FY2014 Performance Budget, Congressional Submission, Federal Prison System, Salaries and Expenses*, p. 3, http://www.justice.gov/jmd/2014justification/pdf/bop-se-justification.pdf.

[62] Ibid., p. 9.

[63] Ibid., p. 8.

Second Chance Act of 2007 (P.L. 110-199) required BOP to develop comprehensive reentry planning for federal inmates.

Office on Violence Against Women (OVW)

The Office on Violence Against Women (OVW) was created to administer programs created under the Violence Against Women Act (VAWA) of 1994 and subsequent legislation. These programs provide financial and technical assistance to communities around the country to facilitate the creation of programs, policies, and practices designed to improve criminal justice responses related to domestic violence, dating violence, sexual assault, and stalking.

For FY2013, the Consolidated and Further Continuing Appropriations Act provided $407.9 million for OVW. For FY2014, the Administration requests $412.5 million for OVW. The House committee-reported bill would provide $413.0 million for this account, and the Senate Committee on Appropriations recommends $417.0 million for the OVW account.

Table 5. Funding for OVW Programs, FY2013 and FY2014

Budget authority in millions of dollars

Program	FY2013 Enacted (Before Sequestration)	FY2014 Request	FY2014 House Committee Reported	FY2014 Senate Committee Reported	FY2014 Enacted
STOP Grants	$185.1	$189.0	$189.0	$193.0	
Research and Evaluation on Violence Against Women	3.4	3.0	3.3	3.0	
Transitional Housing Assistance	24.5	22.0	22.3	25.0	
Grants to Encourage Arrest Policies	49.0	50.0	50.0	50.0	
Homicide Reduction Initiative	(3.9)	(4.0)	(4.0)	(4.0)	
Rural Domestic Violence and Child Abuse Enforcement Assistance Grants	35.7	37.5	35.5	36.0	
Violence on College Campuses	8.8	9.0	9.0	9.0	
Civil Legal Assistance	40.2	41.0	41.0	37.0	
Sexual Assault Victims Services	24.5	23.0	25.0	27.0	
Elder Abuse Grant Program	4.2	4.3	4.3	4.3	
Education and Training for Disabled Female Victims	5.6	5.8	5.8	5.8	
Research on Violence Against Indian Women	1.0	1.0	1.0	1.0	
Consolidated Youth Oriented Program	9.8	10.0	10.0	10.0	
National Resource Center on Workplace Responses	0.5	0.5	0.5	0.5	
Indian Country Sexual Assault Clearinghouse	0.5	0.5	0.5	0.5	

Program	FY2013 Enacted (Before Sequestration)	FY2014 Request	FY2014 House Committee Reported	FY2014 Senate Committee Reported	FY2014 Enacted
Family Civil Justice Program	15.2	—	16.0	15.0	
Enhancing Safety for Victims and their Children in a Family Matter	—	16.0	—	—	
Total: OVW	**407.9**	**412.5**	**413.0**	**417.0**	

Source: The FY2013-enacted amounts (before sequestration) were calculated by CRS. The FY2013-enacted amounts reflect the rescission (1.877%) specified in Section 3001 of the Consolidated and Further Continuing Appropriations Act (P.L. 113-6) and the rescission (0.2%) ordered by OMB per Section 3004 of the act. FY2014 requested amounts were taken from S.Rept. 113-78. The House committee-reported amounts were taken from H.Rept. 113-171 and the Senate committee-reported amounts were taken from S.Rept. 113-78.

Note: Amounts may not add to totals due to rounding.

Office of Justice Programs (OJP)

The Office of Justice Programs (OJP) manages and coordinates the National Institute of Justice, Bureau of Justice Statistics, Office of Juvenile Justice and Delinquency Prevention, Office of Victims of Crimes, Bureau of Justice Assistance, and related grant programs. The Consolidated and Further Continuing Appropriations Act included a total of $1.593 billion for OJP. The Administration's request for OJP for FY2014 is $1.553 billion. The House Committee on Appropriations recommends $1.472 billion for OJP while the Senate Committee on Appropriations recommends $1.642 billion.

Research, Evaluation, and Statistics

The Research, Evaluation, and Statistics account (formerly the Justice Assistance account), among other things, funds the operations of the Bureau of Justice Statistics and the National Institute of Justice. The Consolidated and Further Continuing Appropriations Act included $124.4 million for the Research, Evaluation, and Statistics account. The Administration's FY2014 request for this account is $134.4 million. The House committee-reported bill includes $114.0 million for this account. The Senate Committee on Appropriation recommends $129.0 million for the Research, Evaluation, and Statistics account.

Table 6. Funding for Research, Evaluation, and Statistics, FY2013 and FY2014

Budget authority in millions of dollars

Program	FY2013 Enacted (Before Sequestration)	FY2014 Request	FY2014 House Committee Reported	FY2014 Senate Committee Reported	FY2014 Enacted
Bureau of Justice Statistics	$47.0	$52.9	$42.0	$48.0	
National Institute of Justice	42.1	44.5	37.0	43.0	
Regional Information Sharing System	34.3	25.0	35.0	30.0	
Evaluation Clearinghouse	1.0	3.0	—	2.0	

Program	FY2013 Enacted (Before Sequestration)	FY2014 Request	FY2014 House Committee Reported	FY2014 Senate Committee Reported	FY2014 Enacted
Forensic Science Improvement	—	9.0	—	6.0	
Total: Research, Evaluation, and Statistics	**124.4**	**134.4**	**114.0**	**129.0**	

Source: The FY2013-enacted amounts (before sequestration) were calculated by CRS. The FY2013-enacted amounts reflect the rescission (1.877%) specified in Section 3001 of the Consolidated and Further Continuing Appropriations Act (P.L. 113-6) and the rescission (0.2%) ordered by OMB per Section 3004 of the act. FY2014 requested amounts were taken from S.Rept. 113-78. The House committee-reported amounts were taken from H.Rept. 113-171 and the Senate committee-reported amounts were taken from S.Rept. 113-78.

Note: Amounts may not add to totals due to rounding.

State and Local Law Enforcement Assistance

The State and Local Law Enforcement Assistance account includes funding for a variety of grant programs to improve the functioning of state, local, and tribal criminal justice systems. Some examples of programs that have traditionally been funded under this account include the Edward Byrne Memorial Justice Assistance Grant (JAG) program, the Drug Courts program, the State Criminal Alien Assistance Program (SCAAP), and DNA backlog reduction grants. The State and Local Law Enforcement Assistance account received a total of $1.117 billion under the Consolidated and Further Continuing Appropriations Act. The Administration requests $1.005 billion for this account for FY2014. The House committee-reported bill includes $1.065 billion for State and Local Law Enforcement Assistance while the Senate committee-reported bill includes $1.137 billion.

As a part of the FY2014 request for the State and Local Law Enforcement Assistance account, the Administration proposes to eliminate funding for a variety of programs, including the State Criminal Alien Assistance Program (SCAAP), the border prosecution initiative, the John R. Justice program, the Paul Coverdell Forensic Science program, and the Matching Grant Program for Bulletproof Vests. In its FY2014 congressional budget submission, OJP states that the proposed elimination of these programs is "to ensure that OJP's limited funding is focused on addressing the nation's most important criminal justice priorities."[64] One issue Congress might consider during deliberations of the FY2014 CJS appropriations bill is whether it should adopt the Administration's proposal to eliminate funding for these programs. Both the House and Senate committee-reported bills include funding for SCAAP (see **Table 7**), but the House Appropriation Committee adopted the Administration's proposal to eliminate funding for the John R. Justice program, border prosecution initiatives, Paul Coverdell Forensic Science program, and the Matching Grant Program for Bulletproof Vests. The Senate committee-reported bill includes funding for the John R. Justice program, border prosecution initiatives, the Paul Coverdell Forensic Science program, and the Matching Grant Program for Bulletproof Vests.

The Administration proposes to consolidate funding for the drug and mental health courts into a "problem solving justice" program. The Administration requests $44.0 million for this program.

---

[64] U.S. Department of Justice, Office of Justice Programs, *FY2014 Performance Budget, Office of Justice Programs*, March 2013, p. 26, http://www.justice.gov/jmd/2014justification/pdf/ojp-justification.pdf.

The proposed program would assist state, local, and tribal governments with developing and implementing strategies, including specialized courts, which can divert offenders with drug, mental health, and special needs away from prosecution and incarceration. The proposed program would provide grants, training, and technical assistance to help state, local, and tribal governments develop and implement drug, mental health, and other problem solving courts. As Congress moves forward with its consideration of the CJS appropriations bill, policymakers might consider whether to adopt the Administration's proposal to replace the drug and mental health court programs with the proposed problem solving courts program. Both the House and the Senate Committees on Appropriations rejected the Administration's proposal. Both committees recommended funding for both the drug and mental health court programs.

The Administration requests $85.0 million to expand its Justice Reinvestment Initiative (JRI).[65] The proposed JRI would have three elements:

- It would provide targeted technical assistance to help units of state, local, and tribal governments analyze data on their criminal justice systems, identify what factors are driving prison and jail population growth and develop strategies to reduce costs, improve public safety, reduce unnecessary confinement, and help ex-offenders with the transition back into mainstream society.

- The proposed funding would be used to award implementation grants to the jurisdictions which have adopted significant policy and legislative changes resulting from in-depth data analyses and consensus-based recommendations.

- Funding would also be used to provide incentive grants to participating states to encourage investments in evidence-based criminal justice activities.

OJP reports that 17 states are currently engaged in JRI, a public/private partnership involving OJP's Bureau of Justice Assistance (BJA), the Pew Center on the States, the Vera Institute of Justice, and the Council of State Governments Justice Center. Five states (Kansas, Missouri, Oregon, South Dakota, and West Virginia) are receiving assistance with initial data analysis and policy recommendation development. In the past year, six states (Delaware, Georgia, Hawaii, Louisiana, Oklahoma, and Pennsylvania) have passed criminal justice reform packages and are currently developing detailed implementation plans and requests for implementation funding. An additional six states (Arkansas, Kentucky, New Hampshire, North Carolina, Ohio, and South Carolina) that have previously passed criminal justice reform laws and developed implementation plans have been approved for funding by BJA to implement their plans. The House committee-reported bill includes $25.0 million for JRI while the Senate committee-reported bill includes $30.0 million.

The Administration also requests $50.0 million for the National Criminal History Improvement Program (NCHIP). The NCHIP helps states and territories improve the quality, timeliness, and immediate accessibility of criminal history and related records for use by federal, state, and local law enforcement. According to OJP, "these records play a vital role in supporting criminal investigations, background checks related to firearm purchases, licensing, employment, and the

---

[65] "Justice reinvestment" refers to a data-driven model that (1) develops and implements evidence-based policy options to manage the growth in corrections expenditures; (2) analyzes criminal justice trends to understand the factors that drive jail and prison population growth; (3) reinvests a portion of the savings generated from reducing corrections expenditures into programs to further reduce corrections spending and prevent crime; and (4) measures the effect of the policy changes and reinvestment resources. Ibid., p. 109.

identification of persons subject to protective orders or wanted, arrested, or convicted for stalking and/or domestic violence."[66] The Administration requests $50.0 million for the NCHIP to "provide states [with] stronger incentives to make available several key categories of relevant records and data, including criminal history records and records of persons prohibited from having guns for mental health reasons."[67] If Congress adopts the Administration's proposal it would be the highest funding level for the NCHIP in more than a decade. In addition to the request for NCHIP, the Administration requests $5.0 million for National Instant Criminal Background Check System (NICS) Act Record Improvement Program (NARIP) grants. NARIP grants seeks to "improve the quality of ... background checks and eliminate gaps in records that might allow unauthorized individuals to legally purchase firearms."[68] The House Committee on Appropriations proposes to consolidate NCHIP and NARIP under a proposed "National Instant Criminal Background Check System (NICS) Initiative grants" program. The House committee-reported bill includes $55.0 million for this proposed program. The Senate Committee on Appropriations recommends $50.0 million for NCHIP and $12.0 million for NARIP.

The Administration did not request funding for a tribal assistance grant program for FY2014. However, the Administration's request for OJP includes a proposal to set aside 7% of the amount made available for grant or reimbursement programs under the State and Local Law Enforcement Assistance, Juvenile Justice Programs, and Research, Evaluation, and Statistics accounts for tribal justice assistance. The Senate committee-reported bill includes language that would allow OJP to set aside up to 5% of the amount made available for grant or reimbursement programs under the State and Local Law Enforcement Assistance, Juvenile Justice Programs, and Research, Evaluation, and Statistics accounts for tribal justice assistance. The House committee-reported bill does not include comparable language. Rather, the House Committee on Appropriations recommended $30.0 million under the State and Local Law Enforcement Assistance account for tribal assistance.

Table 7. Funding for State and Local Law Enforcement Assistance Programs, FY2013 and FY2014

Budget authority in millions of dollars

Program	FY2013 Enacted (Before Sequestration)	FY2014 Request	FY2014 House Committee Reported	FY2014 Senate Committee Reported	FY2014 Enacted
Byrne Memorial Justice Assistance Grants	$384.3	$395.0	$465.0	$385.0	
State and Local Intelligence Training	(2.0)	(2.0)	—	(2.0)	
Domestic Radicalization Research	(3.9)	—	(4.0)	—	
Criminal Justice Reform and Recidivism Reduction	(5.9)	—	—	—	

---

[66] Ibid., p. 133.

[67] Ibid.

[68] Ibid., p. 60.

Program	FY2013 Enacted (Before Sequestration)	FY2014 Request	FY2014 House Committee Reported	FY2014 Senate Committee Reported	FY2014 Enacted
State and Local Assistance Help Desk and Diagnostic Center	(3.9)	(2.0)	—	(2.0)	
VALOR Initiative	(4.9)	(15.0)	(15.0)	(15.0)	
Evidence-based Policing Initiative	—	(10.0)	—	(10.0)	
Prosecutorial Decision-making Initiative	—	(5.0)	—	(5.0)	
Voter Education and Plebiscite in Puerto Rico	—	(2.5)	(2.5)	—	
Comprehensive School Safety Initiative	—	—	(75.0)	—	
Byrne Incentive Grants	—	40.0	—	—	
Byrne Competitive Grants	18.6	15.0	10.0	17.0	
John R. Justice Grant Program	3.9	—	—	4.0	
Tribal Assistance	37.3	—	30.0	—	
State Criminal Alien Assistance Program	249.7	—	165.0	190.0	
Border Prosecution Initiatives	4.9	—	—	5.0	
Victims of Trafficking Grants	13.2	10.5	13.5	15.0	
Residential Substance Abuse Treatment	12.2	19.0	6.0	14.0	
Mentally Ill Offenders Act	8.8	—	7.5	9.0	
Drug Courts	40.2	—	41.0	40.0	
Problem Solving Justice Program	—	44.0	—	—	
Veterans' Treatment Courts	3.9	—	4.0	4.0	
Prescription Drug Monitoring	6.9	7.0	7.0	—	
Prison Rape Prevention and Prosecution	12.2	10.5	12.5	—	
Capital Litigation/ Wrongful Conviction Review	2.9	2.0	1.0	3.0	
Missing Alzheimer's Patient Grants	1.0	—	1.0	—	
Economic, High-tech and Cybercrime Prevention	8.8	9.0	4.0	11.0	
CASA-Special Advocates	5.9	—	3.5	6.0	
Second Chance Act	67.3	119.0	55.0	70.5	
Smart Probation	(4.9)	(10.0)	(5.0)	(7.0)	
Children of Incarcerated Parents Demonstration Grants	—	(5.0)	—	(3.0)	

Program	FY2013 Enacted (Before Sequestration)	FY2014 Request	FY2014 House Committee Reported	FY2014 Senate Committee Reported	FY2014 Enacted
Pay for Success	—	(40.0)	—	(15.0)	
Violent Gang and Gun Crime Reduction (Project Safe Neighborhoods)	4.9	5.0	—	17.0	
National Instant Criminal Background Check System Grants	11.8	5.0	—	12.0	
National Criminal History Improvement Program (NCHIP)	5.9	50.0	—	50.0	
National Instant Criminal Background Check System (NICS) Initiative grants	—	—	55.0	—	
Paul Coverdell Forensic Science Grants	11.8	—	—	15.0	
Implementation of the Adam Walsh Act	19.6	20.0	20.0	20.0	
Programs for Children Exposed to Violence	12.7	23.0	—	16.0	
Byrne Criminal Justice Innovation Program	17.6	35.0	—	21.0	
National Sex Offender Public Website	1.0	1.0	1.0	1.0	
Bulletproof Vests Grant Program	21.1	—	—	22.5	
DNA Initiatives	122.4	100.0	125.0	125.0	
Debbie Smith DNA Backlog Grants	(114.6)	—	(117.0)	(117.0)	
Post-conviction DNA Testing Grants	(3.9)	—	(4.0)	(4.0)	
Sexual Assault Nurse Examiners	(3.9)	—	(4.0)	(4.0)	
Rape Kit Backlog Reduction	—	(20.0)	—	—	
Emergency Federal Law Enforcement Assistance	3.4	—	—	—	
Campus Public Safety	2.7	—	3.0	1.0	
Justice Reinvestment Initiative	—	85.0	25.0	30.0	
HOPE Model Implementation Grants	—	10.0	—	8.0	
Vision 21	—	—	—	25.0	
Transfer to DEA for methamphetamine laboratory clean-up	—	—	10.0	—	
Total: State and Local Law Enforcement	**1,116.8**	**1,005.0**	**1,065.0**	**1,137.0**	

Juvenile Justice Programs

The Juvenile Justice Programs account includes funding for grant programs to reduce juvenile delinquency and help state, local, and tribal governments improve the functioning of their juvenile justice systems.

The Consolidated and Further Continuing Appropriations Act provided $273.7 million for juvenile justice programs. The Administration's FY2014 request includes $332.5 million for juvenile justice programs. Within this request, the Administration is requesting additional funding for existing programs as well as to establish new programs and initiatives. For instance, the Administration is requesting additional funding for the Title V Incentive Grants to establish the Juvenile Justice Education Collaboration Assistance (JJECA) initiative. This initiative would, among other things, provide funding for evidence-based practices and programs to create positive school environments (including in correctional education settings) and enhance student behavior and academic success. The Administration is also proposing a competitive grant focusing on the gender-specific needs of girls in the juvenile justice system. The FY2014 request also includes funding for a proposed Juvenile Justice Realignment Incentive Grants program to provide competitive grants to states that use their Juvenile Accountability Block Grant (JABG) funding for evidence-based programs. In addition, the FY2014 request includes funding for a projected web portal to support children of incarcerated parents.

The House Committee on Appropriations recommends $196.0 million for Juvenile Justice Programs. This proposal would eliminate funding for a number of programs including the Title V Incentive Grants program and the JABG program. The Senate committee-reported bill would provide $279.0 million for this account.

Table 8. Funding for Juvenile Justice Programs, FY2013 and FY2014

Budget authority in millions of dollars

Program	FY2013 Enacted (Before Sequestration)	FY2014 Request	FY2014 House Committee Reported	FY2014 Senate Committee Reported	FY2014 Enacted
Part B—State Formula	$43.1	$70.0	$20.0	$50.0	
Emergency Planning—Juvenile Detention Facilities	0.5	—	—	0.5	
Youth Mentoring Grants	88.1	58.0	90.0	61.0	
Title V—Incentive Grants	19.6	56.0	—	35.0	
Tribal Youth	(9.8)	—	—	(10.0)	
Gang Prevention	(4.9)	—	—	(5.0)	
Alcohol Use Prevention	(4.9)	—	—	(5.0)	

Program	FY2013 Enacted (Before Sequestration)	FY2014 Request	FY2014 House Committee Reported	FY2014 Senate Committee Reported	FY2014 Enacted
Juvenile Justice and Education Collaboration Assistance	—	(20.0)	—	(10.0)	
Juvenile Justice Realignment Incentive Grants	—	—	—	(5.0)	
Investigation and Prosecution of Child Abuse Programs	18.6	—	19.0	19.0	
Juvenile Accountability Block Grants	24.5	30.0	—	30.0	
Juvenile Justice Realignment Incentive Grants	—	20.0	—	—	
Community-based Violence Prevention Initiative	10.8	25.0	—	11.0	
Training for Judicial Personnel	1.5	—	—	1.5	
Missing and Exploited Children Programs	65.6	67.0	67.0	67.0	
National Forum on Youth Violence Prevention	2.0	4.0	—	2.0	
Competitive Grants Focusing on Girls in the Juvenile Justice System	—	2.0	—	2.0	
Children of Incarcerated Parents Web Portal	—	0.5	—	0.5	
Total: Juvenile Justice Programs	**273.7**	**332.5**	**196.0**	**279.0**	

Source: The FY2013-enacted amounts (before sequestration) were calculated by CRS. The FY2013-enacted amounts reflect the rescission (1.877%) specified in Section 3001 of the Consolidated and Further Continuing Appropriations Act (P.L. 113-6) and the rescission (0.2%) ordered by OMB per Section 3004 of the act. FY2014 requested amounts were taken from S.Rept. 113-78. The House committee-reported amounts were taken from H.Rept. 113-171 and the Senate committee-reported amounts were taken from S.Rept. 113-78.

Note: Amounts may not add to totals due to rounding.

Public Safety Officers Benefits Program (PSOB)

The Public Safety Officers Benefits (PSOB) program provides three different types of benefits to public safety officers and their survivors: death, disability, and education. The PSOB program is intended to assist in the recruitment and retention of law enforcement officers, firefighters, and first responders and to offer peace of mind to men and women who choose careers in public safety. The Consolidated and Further Continuing Appropriations Act provided $78.0 million for PSOB. The Administration requests $97.3 million for this account for FY2014. Both the House and the Senate Appropriations Committees recommend funding the PSOB program at a level equal to the Administration's request.

Community Oriented Policing Services (COPS)

The Community Oriented Policing Services (COPS) Office awards grants to state, local, and tribal law enforcement agencies throughout the United States so they can hire and train law enforcement officers to participate in community policing, purchase and deploy new crime-fighting technologies, and develop and test new and innovative policing strategies. The COPS program received $217.9 million under the Consolidated and Further Continuing Appropriations Act. The Administration requests $439.5 million for this account for FY2014. The House Committee on Appropriations recommends eliminating the COPS account. The Senate Committee on Appropriations recommends $393.5 million for this account.

The Administration's FY2014 request for COPS includes $150.0 million for a proposed comprehensive schools safety program. The proposed program would provide funding for hiring school safety personnel, including school resource officers, civilian public safety positions, school psychologists, social workers, and counselors. Funding would also be available for purchasing school safety equipment; developing and updating public safety plans; conducting threat assessments; and training crisis intervention teams. The stated purpose of the program is to "bring the law enforcement, mental health, and education disciplines together to provide a comprehensive approach to school safety."[69] The Administration reports that the program would require law enforcement and school districts, in consultation with school mental health professionals, to apply for funding together and use the grant to fill the gaps in their own school safety and security efforts. The House committee-reported bill includes $75.0 million for the proposed school safety program as a set aside from appropriations for the Edward Byrne Memorial Justice Assistance Grant (JAG) program (see **Table 7**). Language in H.Rept. 113-171 directs the National Institute of Justice to develop and implement the school safety program. The Senate Committee on Appropriations includes $150.0 million for the proposed program under the COPS account (see **Table 9**).

Table 9. Funding for Community Oriented Policing Services Programs, FY2013 and FY2014

Budget authority in millions of dollars

Program	FY2013 Enacted (Before Sequestration)	FY2014 Request	FY2014 House Committee Reported	FY2014 Senate Committee Reported	FY2014 Enacted
COPS Hiring Program	$186.1	$257.0	—	$201.0	
Transfer to the Tribal Resources Grant Program	(14.7)	(15.0)	—	(15.0)	
Transfer for Community Policing Development	(9.8)	(15.0)	—	(10.0)	
Training and Technical Assistance on the Collaborative Reform Model	—	(10.0)	—	(5.0)	

---

[69] U.S. Department of Justice, Community Oriented Policing Services Office, *FY2014 Performance Budget, Office of Community Oriented Policing Services*, March 2013, p. 26, http://www.justice.gov/jmd/2014justification/pdf/cops-justification.pdf.

Program	FY2013 Enacted (Before Sequestration)	FY2014 Request	FY2014 House Committee Reported	FY2014 Senate Committee Reported	FY2014 Enacted
Transfer to the Drug Enforcement Administration for Clandestine Methamphetamine Lab Clean-up	12.2	12.5	—a	12.5	
Tribal Resources Grant Program	19.6	20.0	—	20.0	
Comprehensive School Safety Program	—	150.0	—a	150.0	
Anti-methamphetamine Task Forces	—	—	—	10.0	
Total: Community Oriented Policing Services	**217.9**	**439.5**	**—**	**393.5**	

Source: The FY2013-enacted amounts (before sequestration) were calculated by CRS. The FY2013-enacted amounts reflect the rescission (1.877%) specified in Section 3001 of the Consolidated and Further Continuing Appropriations Act (P.L. 113-6) and the rescission (0.2%) ordered by OMB per Section 3004 of the act. FY2014 requested amounts were taken from S.Rept. 113-78. The House committee-reported amounts were taken from H.Rept. 113-171 and the Senate committee-reported amounts were taken from S.Rept. 113-78.

Note: Amounts may not add to totals due to rounding.

a. See **Table 7**.

The Crime Victims Fund

The Crime Victims Fund (CVF) was established by the Victims of Crime Act of 1984 (P.L. 98-473, VOCA). It is administered by the Office for Victims of Crime (OVC), and provides funding to the states and territories for victim compensation and assistance programs. This account does not receive appropriations (thus the amount for the CVF is not included in **Table 4**) but instead is largely funded by criminal fines, forfeited bail bonds, penalties, and special assessments that are collected by U.S. Attorneys' Offices, U.S. courts, and the BOP.[70]

For FY2013, the Consolidated and Further Continuing Appropriations Act set the obligation limit at $730.0 million. For FY2014, the Administration requests that the obligation limit on the Crime Victims Fund be set at $800.0 million. In the FY2014 request, the Administration specifies that $45.0 million is for the Vision 21 Initiative, and $10.0 million is for Victims of Trafficking Grants. Of the $45.0 million for Vision 21, $20.0 million is allotted for Tribal Assistance for Victims of Violence and $25.0 million is allotted for additional victims' services and initiatives. The House committee-reported bill would set the CVF obligation limit at 745.0 million. The House Committee on Appropriations specifies that OVC may implement Vision 21[71] within

---

[70] U.S. Department of Justice, Office for Victims of Crime, *About OVC, Crime Victims Fund*, http://www.ojp.usdoj.gov/ovc/about/victimsfund html.

[71] Vision 21 is a strategic planning initiative based on an 18-month national assessment by OVC that assesses current and emerging challenges and opportunities facing the field. The initiative addresses identified needs, including the need for more victim related data, research and program evaluation; legal assistance for crime victims; resources for tribal victims; and other related assistance. Of the $45.0 million requested for Vision 21, $20.0 million will be used to support Tribal Assistance for Victims of Violence and $25.0 million will be used for additional victims' services and initiatives. For more information, see U.S. Department of Justice, Office of Justice Programs, *FY2014 Performance Budget*, http://www.justice.gov/jmd/2014justification/pdf/ojp-justification.pdf.

available resources. The Senate Committee on Appropriations recommends $765.0 million for the obligation limit and proposes $25.0 million in support of the Vision 21 Initiative; however, the Senate committee-reported bill would provide funding for Vision 21 through discretionary sources instead of the CVF (see **Table 7**).

Science Agencies[72]

The Science Agencies fund and otherwise support research and development (R&D) and related activities across a wide variety of federal missions, including national competitiveness, energy and the environment, and fundamental discovery.

FY2013 and FY2014 Appropriations

The Consolidated and Further Continuing Appropriations Act provides $24.737 billion in post-rescission FY2013 funding for the Science Agencies. This funding level does not incorporate reductions due to the effects of sequestration as mandated by the Budget Control Act of 2011 (P.L. 112-25). The Administration requests a total of $25.347 billion for the Science Agencies. The House Committee on Appropriations recommends a total of $23.599 billion for the science agencies. The Senate committee-reported bill would provide a total of $25.442 billion for the science agencies.

Table 10. Funding for Science Agencies, FY2013 and FY2014

Budget authority in millions of dollars

Accounts	FY2013 Enacted (Before Sequestration)	FY2014 Request	FY2014 House Committee Reported	FY2014 Senate Committee Reported	FY2014 Enacted
Office of Science and Technology Policy	$5.7	$5.7	$5.5	$5.7	
National Aeronautics and Space Administration	17,506.7a	17,715.4	16,598.3	18,010.3	
National Science Foundation	7,239.8	7,625.8	6,995.1	7,425.9	
Total: Science Agencies	**24,752.2**	**25,346.8**	**23,598.9**	**25,441.8**	

Source: FY2013-enacted (before sequestration) and FY2014-requested amounts were taken from S.Rept. 113-78. The FY2013-enacted amounts include the rescissions specified in Sections 3001 of the Consolidated and Further Continuing Appropriations Act (P.L. 113-6) and the rescissions ordered by OMB pursuant to Section 3004 of the act. The FY2013-enacted amounts also include supplemental appropriations for the CJS departments and agencies included in the Disaster Relief Appropriations Act, 2013 (P.L. 113-2). The House committee-reported amounts were taken from H.Rept. 113-171; the Senate committee-reported amounts were taken from S.Rept. 113-78.

Note: Amounts may not add to totals due to rounding.

---

[72] This section was coordinated by John F. Sargent, Jr., Specialist in Science and Technology Policy, CRS Resources, Science, and Industry Division.

a. This amount includes $15.0 million in supplemental funding for the National Aeronautics and Space Administration.

Office of Science and Technology Policy (OSTP)[73]

Congress established the Office of Science and Technology Policy (OSTP) through the National Science and Technology Policy, Organization, and Priorities Act of 1976 (P.L. 94-282). The act states that "the primary function of the OSTP director is to provide, within the Executive Office of the President, advice on the scientific, engineering, and technological aspects of issues that require attention at the highest level of Government." The OSTP director, often referred to informally as the President's science advisor, also manages the National Science and Technology Council (NSTC),[74] which coordinates science and technology policy across the executive branch of the federal government, and co-chairs the President's Council of Advisors on Science and Technology (PCAST),[75] a council of external advisors that provides advice to the President on matters related to science and technology policy. OSTP is one of two offices in the Executive Office of the President (EOP) that is funded in the CJS appropriations bill.[76]

The Consolidated and Further Continuing Appropriations Act included $5.7 million for OSTP. For FY2014, the Administration requests $5.7 million. The House Committee on Appropriations would provide $5.5 million for OSTP. The Senate Committee on Appropriations recommends $5.7 million.

According to the Administration, its request would "restore funding to levels that enables [sic] OSTP to carry out its significant national security emergency preparedness communications responsibilities that must be performed in times of national crisis," and support the director of OSTP, the federal Chief Technology Officer, three Senate-confirmed associate directors, and other professional staff members.[77]

Congress has for several years restricted OSTP from engaging in certain activities with China or any Chinese-owned company by prohibiting the use of appropriated funds for these activities. The OSTP may proceed with activities that it certifies pose no risk of transferring technology or information with security implications to China and will not involve knowing interactions with officials who have been determined by the United States to have direct involvement with violations of human rights. Such certification must be submitted to the House and Senate Committees at least 30 days prior to such activities. Congress may continue its interest in the debate over its ability to restrict the activities of OSTP and the scope of such restrictions. The House-reported bill would extend the current restrictions on OSTP use of funds to "develop, design, plan, promulgate, implement, or execute a bilateral policy, program, order, or contract of any kind to participate, collaborate, or coordinate bilaterally in any way with China or any Chinese-owned company." The Senate-reported bill lacks comparable language.

---

[73] This section was prepared by Dana A. Shea, Specialist in Science and Technology Policy, Resources, Science, and Industry Division.

[74] Executive Order 12881 established the National Science and Technology Council.

[75] Executive Order 13539 established the President's Council of Advisors on Science and Technology.

[76] The other EOP office funded under the CJS appropriations bill is the Office of the United States Trade Representative.

[77] Executive Office of the President, *Executive Office of the President, Fiscal Year 2014 Congressional Budget Submission*, April 2013, http://www.whitehouse.gov/sites/default/files/docs/2014-eop-budget1_0.pdf.

In its FY2014 budget, the Administration proposes a reorganization of federal STEM education programs. The explanatory statement for P.L. 113-6 directed OSTP to produce a federal STEM education strategic plan within 45 days of enactment of the law. According to OSTP, the strategy document informed the proposed reorganization plan, though OSTP had not yet published the strategy document at the time of the President's FY2014 budget release.[78] The National Science and Technology Council released the federal STEM education strategic plan on May 31, 2013.[79] Neither the House nor Senate committee supports the proposed reorganization. In addition, the House committee identifies flaws in the subsequent federal STEM strategic plan, including the proposed mechanism for dissemination of federal STEM education research and findings. The House committee would direct OSTP to report within 180 days of passage on the resources and authorities necessary to develop a "one stop" style website containing findings from federal research on STEM education. The Senate committee report would defer action on such consolidation until OSTP finalizes STEM program assessments and require OSTP to work with non-federal education and outreach communities on any subsequent reorganization proposal.

In February 2013, OSTP directed federal agencies with more than $100 million in research and development expenditures to "develop plans to make the published results of federally funded research freely available to the public within one year of publication and requiring researchers to better account for and manage the digital data resulting from federally funded scientific research."[80] Both committee reports address this new policy. The House report would direct OSTP to report semiannually to the committee on the status of agencies' plan development and implementation. The Senate report would direct OSTP to report to the committee and appropriate authorizing committees regarding the Administration's coordinated plan to support increased public access as well as implementation guidelines across the affected agencies and scientific disciplines.

The House report also expresses support for OSTP-mediated federal agency collaboration on neuroscience and would encourage OSTP to report to the committee semi-annually on its efforts in this area. The House report also expresses support for OSTP efforts to reassess and update the criticality of strategic mineral supply chains. The House report urges leverage of these results into an interagency plan to reduce dependence on foreign sources and would direct OSTP to report to the committee regarding the results of these efforts.

The Consolidated and Further Continuing Appropriations Act, 2013, included $2.8 million for the Science and Technology Policy Institute (STPI), a federally funded research and development center that supports OSTP. The National Science Foundation requests $4.9 million in FY2014 funding for STPI. Of this $4.9 million, $1.5 million is to support OSTP leadership, in coordination with the U.S. Group on Earth Observations Subcommittee of the NSTC, of a new interagency Big Earth Data initiative to improve coordination and management of federal Earth system observations, data, and information.

---

[78] Personal communication between CRS and OSTP, April 12, 2013.

[79] National Science and Technology Council, Executive Office of the President, *Federal Science, Technology, Education, and Mathematics (STEM) Education 5-Year Strategic Plan*, May 31, 2013, http://www.whitehouse.gov/sites/default/files/microsites/ostp/stem_stratplan_2013.pdf.

[80] Office of Science and Technology Policy, Executive Office of the President, "Increasing Access to the Results of Federally Funded Scientific Research," *Memorandum for the Heads of Executive Departments and Agencies*, February 22, 2013.

National Aeronautics and Space Administration (NASA)[81]

The National Aeronautics and Space Administration (NASA) was created by the 1958 National Aeronautics and Space Act (P.L. 85-568) to conduct civilian space and aeronautics activities. The agency is managed from headquarters in Washington, DC. It has nine major field centers around the country, plus the Jet Propulsion Laboratory, which is operated under contract by the California Institute of Technology.

The Administration has requested $17.715 billion for NASA for FY2014. The FY2013 appropriation (after rescissions, but before sequestration) was $17.507 billion.[82] For FY2014, the House committee recommends $16.598 billion, while the Senate committee recommends $18.010 billion. See **Table 11** for a breakdown of these amounts by appropriations account. There is no authorized level for NASA funding in FY2014; the most recent authorization act (the NASA Authorization Act of 2010, P.L. 111-267) authorized appropriations through FY2013.[83]

The FY2014 request for Science is $5.018 billion. The FY2013 appropriation (after rescissions, but before sequestration) was $5.037 billion. The House and Senate committees recommend $4.781 billion and $5.154 billion respectively.

Within the Science account, the request for Planetary Science ($1.218 billion) includes $40.5 million for observation of near-Earth objects and $50 million for management of a Department of Energy (DOE) program to produce plutonium-238, which some spacecraft use for power generation. In the past, congressional policymakers have disagreed about whether NASA or DOE should fund DOE production of plutonium-238 for NASA. The House and Senate committee recommendations for Planetary Science are respectively $1.315 billion and $1.318 billion. Among other differences relative to the request, the House committee recommends increases for exploration of Mars and the outer planets and no funding for plutonium-238 production. The Senate committee's recommended increase is entirely for Mars exploration.

Also in the Science account, the request for Earth Science is $1.846 billion. The FY2013 appropriation for Earth Science (after rescissions, but before sequestration) was $1.748 billion. The Earth Science request includes $30 million to begin development of future land imaging capabilities to replace the current Landsat satellites, operated by the U.S. Geological Survey, as well as funds to assume responsibility for certain Earth-observing satellite instruments previously held by the National Oceanographic and Atmospheric Administration (NOAA). The House committee recommends $1.659 billion for Earth Science, and its report states that no funds should be spent on the proposed Landsat and NOAA-related activities. The Senate committee recommends approximately the requested amount for Earth Science, including the requested funds for land imaging, but its report expresses concern about the Administration's approach and directs NASA to submit a plan for implementing future Landsat satellites at substantially lower cost.

The request for the James Webb Space Telescope (JWST), also funded in the Science account, is $658.2 million. NASA expects FY2014 to be the peak funding year for JWST and states that the

---

[81] This section was prepared by Daniel Morgan, Specialist in Science and Technology Policy, Resources, Science, and Industry Division.

[82] Includes $15 million in supplemental funding provided by the Disaster Relief Appropriations Act, 2013 (P.L. 113-2).

[83] Bills that would authorize FY2014 appropriations for NASA include H.R. 2687, H.R. 2616, and S. 1317.

budget and schedule for the JWST program remain consistent with the 2011 revised plan. In the FY2012 appropriations conference report, Congress capped the formulation and development cost of JWST and mandated annual reports on the program by the Government Accountability Office. The House committee recommends $584.0 million for JWST in FY2014. The Senate committee recommends the requested amount.

The request for Aeronautics is $565.7 million. The FY2013 appropriation (after rescissions, but before sequestration) was $558.2 million. The request for Integrated Systems Research includes a new program on advanced composite materials and structures. In the Fundamental Aeronautics program, NASA plans to explore options for the future of its rotorcraft research; this planning will be coordinated with other government agencies and industry partners. The House committee recommends $566.0 million for Aeronautics, while the Senate committee recommends $558.7 million.

For Space Technology, the Administration has requested $742.6 million. The FY2013 appropriation (after rescissions, but before sequestration) was $628.7 million. The requested increase would support existing projects that are moving from the planning and design phase to the more expensive tasks of hardware manufacture and demonstration. The request also includes funds to accelerate the development of high-power solar electric propulsion technology for future spacecraft. The House and Senate committee recommendations are respectively $576.0 million and $670.1 million.

The Administration's request for Exploration in FY2014 is $3.916 billion. The FY2013 appropriation (after rescissions, but before sequestration) was $3.806 billion. This account funds development of the Orion Multipurpose Crew Vehicle (MPCV) and the Space Launch System (SLS) heavy-lift rocket, mandated by the 2010 authorization act for human exploration beyond Earth orbit. The account also funds development of a commercial crew transportation capability for future U.S. astronaut access to the International Space Station. The request of $821.4 million for commercial crew is more than the FY2013 appropriation, while the request of $2.730 billion for Orion, the SLS, and related ground systems (known collectively as Exploration Systems Development) is less than the FY2013 appropriation. In the past, this apparent difference in human spaceflight priorities between Congress and the Administration has been controversial. According to NASA, the amounts requested are consistent with the planned schedules for both Orion/SLS and commercial crew. NASA officials state that the request for commercial crew is necessary to make commercial crew transportation services available in 2017, while the request for Orion and SLS is sufficient for an uncrewed flight of the SLS in 2017 and a crewed flight in 2021. The House committee recommends $3.612 billion, including $500 million for commercial crew and $2.825 billion for Exploration Systems Development. The Senate committee recommends $4.209 billion, including $775 million for commercial crew and $3.118 billion for Exploration Systems Development.

The FY2014 request for Space Operations is $3.883 billion. The FY2013 appropriation (after rescissions, but before sequestration) was $3.871 billion. The Space Operations account funds the International Space Station (ISS) and the Space and Flight Support program. The House committee recommends $3.670 billion, while the Senate committee recommends the requested amount.

The request for Education is $94.2 million. The FY2013 appropriation (after rescissions, but before sequestration) was $122.4 million. NASA education programs are being consolidated as part of a government-wide reorganization of programs in science, technology, engineering, and mathematics (STEM) education. Among the programs included in the FY2014 request for the Education account are the National Space Grant College and Fellowship Program ($24 million), the Experimental Program to Stimulate Competitive Research (EPSCoR, $9 million), and the Minority University Research Education Program (MUREP, $30 million). In the past, other NASA accounts also funded some education activities; in most cases, these additional education funds are not included in the FY2014 request for those accounts. The House committee recommends $122.0 million for Education, including the requested amounts for Space Grant, EPSCoR, and MUREP. The House report mandates the internal consolidation of NASA education activities, whereby the Education account would be NASA's "exclusive source of appropriated funds for education and public outreach activities"; it states that this would improve coordination, efficiency, and accountability and reduce fragmentation. The Senate committee recommends $116.6 million for Education, including $40 million for Space Grant, $18 million for EPSCoR, and $30 million for MUREP. The Senate report states that while the committee encourages the streamlining and consolidation of education activities within NASA, it does not support the Administration's proposal to terminate certain NASA education activities in order to fund additional STEM education activities at other agencies.

The Administration has proposed a NASA mission to capture a small asteroid robotically, redirect it into orbit around the Moon, and explore it with astronauts as one of the first destinations for Orion and the SLS. The FY2014 budget request includes initial funding for this mission in three different accounts: $20 million in Science for identification and characterization of a suitable asteroid, $45 million in Exploration for mission definition and planning and development of capture mechanisms, and $40 million in Space Technology for development of the solar electric propulsion technology that would be used to redirect the asteroid's orbit. The House report calls the proposed asteroid mission "premature" and states that the House committee's recommendation "does not include any of the requested increases associated with the asteroid retrieval proposal."

Table 11. Funding for NASA, FY2013 and FY2014

Budget authority in millions of dollars

Accounts	FY2013 Enacted (Before Sequestration)	FY2014 Request	FY2014 House Committee Reported	FY2014 Senate Committee Reported	FY2014 Enacted
Science	$5,037.4	$5,017.8	$4,781.0	$5,154.2	
Aeronautics	558.2	565.7	566.0	558.7	
Space Technology	628.7	742.6	576.0	670.1	
Exploration	3,806.4	3,915.5	3,612.0	4,209.3	
Space Operations	3,871.0	3,882.9	3,670.0	3,882.9	
Education	122.4	94.2	122.0	116.6	
Cross-Agency Support	2,764.5	2,850.3	2,711.0	2,793.6	
Construction and Environmental Compliance and Restoration	680.9a	609.4	525.0	586.9	
Inspector General	37.2	37.0	35.3	38.0	
Total: NASA	**17,506.7**	**17,715.4**	**16,598.3**	**18,010.3**	

Sources: FY2013-enacted (before sequestration) and FY2014-requested amounts were taken from S.Rept. 113-78. The FY2013-enacted amounts include the rescissions specified in Section 3001 of the Consolidated and Further Continuing Appropriations Act (P.L. 113-6) and the rescissions ordered by OMB pursuant to Section 3004 of the act. The FY2013-enacted amounts also include supplemental appropriations in the Disaster Relief Appropriations Act, 2013 (P.L. 113-2). The House committee-reported amounts were taken from H.Rept. 113-171, and the Senate committee-reported amounts were taken from S.Rept. 113-78.

Note: Amounts may not add to totals due to rounding.

a.   This amount includes $15.0 million in supplemental funding.

National Science Foundation (NSF)[84]

The National Science Foundation (NSF) supports basic research and education in the non-medical sciences and engineering. Congress established the foundation as an independent federal agency in 1950 and directed it to "promote the progress of science; to advance the national health, prosperity, and welfare; to secure the national defense; and for other purposes."[85] The NSF is a primary source of federal support for U.S. university research. It is also responsible for significant shares of the federal science, technology, engineering, and mathematics (STEM) education program portfolio and federal STEM student aid and support.

For FY2014 the Administration seeks $7.626 billion in funding for the NSF. NSF indicates that its overarching priorities for FY2014 include six programs: Cyber-enabled Materials, Manufacturing, and Smart Systems (CEMMS, $300.4 million); Cyberinfrastructure Framework for 21st Century Science, Engineering, and Education (CIF21, $155.5 million); NSF Innovation Corps (I-Corps, $24.9 million); Integrated NSF Support Promoting Interdisciplinary Research and Education (INSPIRE, $63.0 million); Science, Engineering, and Education for Sustainability (SEES, $222.8 million); and Secure and Trustworthy Cyberspace (SaTC, $110.3 million). Congress did not specify funding for these individual accounts in the Consolidated and Further Continuing Appropriations Act. P.L. 113-6 provided $7.240 billion (after rescissions, but before sequestration) in appropriations to NSF in FY2013.[86] Congress has not enacted specific funding authorization levels for NSF in FY2014.[87]

The House Committee on Appropriations recommends a total of $6.995 billion for NSF in FY2014. The Senate Committee on Appropriations recommends a total of $7.426 billion.

Since FY2006, overall increases in the NSF budget have been at least partially driven by the so-called "doubling path policy." Congress and successive Administrations have sought to double funding for the NSF, Department of Energy's Office of Science, and National Institute of Standards and Technology's core laboratory and construction accounts (collectively "the targeted accounts").[88] However, actual funding for the targeted accounts has generally not reached authorized levels during the authorization period, which ends in FY2013. It is unclear if Congress

[84] This section was prepared by Heather B. Gonzalez, Specialist in Science and Technology Policy, Resources, Science, and Industry Division.

[85] The National Science Foundation Act of 1950 (P.L. 81-507), Purpose.

[86] All FY2013 funding levels for NSF in this section have been adjusted to reflect the enacted level minus the rescissions authorized by P.L. 113-6, Sections 3001 and 3004. They do not reflect the effects of the sequestration or other potential changes to budget authority for FY2013.

[87] The FY2014 NSF budget refers to the foundation's organic act, P.L. 81-507, for general budgetary authority.

[88] For an analysis of the doubling effort that includes historic trends, see CRS Report R41951, *An Analysis of Efforts to Double Federal Funding for Physical Sciences and Engineering Research*, by John F. Sargent Jr.

will seek to continue the doubling path policy in FY2014. Previous Administration budgets and supporting documents have stated the President's intention to double funding for these accounts; the President's FY2014 budget and supporting documents express support for increasing basic research at these agencies, but does not expressly commit to a doubling effort. In FY2013 some legislators raised concerns about pursuing the doubling effort given the nation's fiscal challenges, including one who urged observers "to be realistic about the notion of doubling the NSF budget."- Other analysts have asserted that without the doubling path policy in place, funding levels for targeted accounts might have fallen over the past half-decade.[89]

Congress typically appropriates to NSF at the major account level. NSF's major accounts are Research and Related Activities (R&RA), Education and Human Resources (E&HR), Major Research Equipment and Facilities Construction (MREFC), Agency Operations and Awards Management (AOAM), the National Science Board (NSB), and the Office of Inspector General (IG). In some cases, such as the Graduate Research Fellowship (GRF), program funding may come from two or more of these accounts.

R&RA is the largest NSF account and the primary source of research funding at the NSF. The Administration seeks $6.212 billion in funding for R&RA in FY2014 noting "strong support for cross-cutting research priorities such as advanced manufacturing, clean energy and sustainability, break-through materials, robotics, cyberinfrastructure, and cybersecurity."[90] NSF consolidated certain R&RA sub-accounts in FY2013, moving from 11 directorates and offices to 8.[91] P.L. 113-6 provided $5.859 billion (after rescissions, but before sequestration) in funding for R&RA in FY2013.

The House Committee on Appropriations recommends $5.676 billion for R&RA in FY2014. The Senate Committee on Appropriations recommends $6.018 billion. The House report[92] provides $13.9 million for new investments in cognitive science and neuroscience research, offers the requested levels for various (unspecified) R&RA advanced manufacturing proposals, and supports a temporary reduction in Antarctic research funding in order to provide funds for the implementation of certain recommended safety and management changes. The Senate report[93] directs NSF to apply the $194.0 million reduction to R&RA (from the requested level) to the so-called OneNSF initiatives.[94] Among other things, the Senate report also provides the full request for SEES ($222.8 million).

The FY2014 request for R&RA's Experimental Program to Stimulate Competitive Research (EPSCoR) program is $163.6 million. The explanatory statement that accompanied P.L. 113-6 (hereinafter referred to as the "explanatory statement") provided $154.9 million (after rescissions,

---

[89] Testimony of Dr. Jeffrey L. Furman, in U.S. Congress, Senate Committee on Commerce, Science, and Transportation, "Five Years of the America COMPETES Act: Progress, Challenges, and Next Steps," hearings, 112th Cong., 2nd sess., September 19, 2012.

[90] National Science Foundation, *FY2014 Budget Request to Congress*, April 10, 2013, p. R&RA-1.

[91] See table note "a" in **Table 12**.

[92] This section refers to H.Rept. 113-171, which accompanied H.R. 2787 (Commerce, Justice, Science, and Related Agencies Appropriations Bill, 2014) when it was reported from committee, as the "House report."

[93] This section refers to S.Rept. 113-78, which accompanied S. 1329 (Commerce and Justice, and Science, and Related Agencies Appropriations Bill, 2014) when it was reported from committee, as the "Senate report."

[94] It is not clear how this directive might be applied in practice. The FY2014 budget request does not include the term "OneNSF." However, NSF described the six programs identified as "FY2014 Priorities" in its FY2014 budget request as "OneNSF" initiatives in its FY2013 budget request.

---

but before sequestration) for EPSCoR in FY2013.[95] The Senate report provides $163.6 million to EPSCoR in FY2014. The House report is silent on the question of FY2014 funding for EPSCoR.

The Administration seeks $880.3 million in funding for E&HR in FY2014. E&HR is the primary source of funding for science, technology, engineering, and mathematics (STEM) education at the NSF. P.L. 113-6 provided $877.0 million (after rescissions, but before sequestration) in funding for E&HR in FY2013. The House Committee on Appropriations recommends $825.0 million for E&HR in FY2014. The Senate Committee on Appropriations recommends $880.3 million.

For FY2014 the Administration proposes a reorganization and consolidation of many federal STEM education programs.[96] Under the Administration's plan, NSF would play a leadership role in the federal undergraduate and graduate STEM education efforts. (The Department of Education and Smithsonian Institution would focus on K-12 education and informal STEM education, respectively.) The House and Senate reports both reject the proposed reorganization plan for programs within the purview of the FY2014 Commerce, Justice, Science, and Related Agencies appropriations act. The House report notes that there may be individual instances in which the Committee accepts a change. The Senate report defers action on the reorganization until the Office of Science and Technology Policy (OSTP) finalizes STEM education program assessments as required by the America COMPETES Reauthorization Act of 2010 (P.L. 111-358).

The foundation's FY2014 budget request for E&HR highlights several changes associated with the Administration's plan for STEM education: establishment of the Catalyzing Advances in Undergraduate STEM Education (CAUSE) program;[97] expansion of the GRF to serve the whole of the federal enterprise;[98] and creation of the NSF Research Traineeship (NRT), which would replace the Integrative Graduate Education Research Traineeship (IGERT).[99] The House report specifically rejects the establishment of the CAUSE program or the change to a federal

---

[95] See, Senator Barbara Mikulski, "Consolidated and Further Continuing Appropriations Act," *Congressional Record*, daily edition, vol. 159, part 34 (March 11, 2013), pp. S1287-S1587.

[96] The Administration indicates that it plans to reduce the number of federal STEM education programs by about 50% and to shift approximately $180.0 million in budget authority from various federal agencies to the NSF, Department of Education, and Smithsonian. Some programs within these three receiving agencies would be consolidated, as would STEM education programs at other federal agencies.

[97] The CAUSE program would consolidate three E&HR undergraduate programs, three R&RA education programs, and one NSF-wide program. The E&HR programs are: the STEM Talent Expansion Program (STEP), Widening Implementation and Demonstration of Evidence-Based Reforms (WIDER), and Transforming Undergraduate Education in STEM (TUES). The R&RA programs, along with their respective directorates, are: Transforming Undergraduate Biology Education (TUBE, Biological Sciences), Research in Engineering Education and Nanotechnology Undergraduate Education (NUE, Engineering), and Geosciences Education and Opportunities for Enhancing Diversity in the Geosciences (OEDG, Geosciences). The NSF-wide program is the Climate Change Education (CCE) program. The Administration seeks $123.1 million in funding for CAUSE in FY2014.

[98] The Administration's proposed changes to the GRF would make NSF a central source for all federal STEM fellowships. Under the plan, the GRF would become the National Graduate Research Fellowship (NGRF) program. Budget authority for certain federal fellowships at other federal agencies would be reduced and funding for the NGRF would be increased. NSF would consult with its directorates, as well as with other federal agencies, to ensure that "suitable targeted opportunities are provided." It is unclear how this consolidation might affect the distribution of fellowships across various STEM fields. The FY2014 budget request for the NGRF is $325.1 million. NSF asserts that this level of funding will provide for an increase of approximately 700 fellows, for a total of 2,700 new fellowships in FY2014.

[99] The Administration seeks to eliminate the IGERT in FY2014 and to replace it with the NRT. The FY2014 NSF budget request states that the NRT will "build on what has been learned through IGERT, the Graduate STEM Fellows in K-12 Education (GK-12) program, and in other relevant NSF-sponsored efforts." The GK-12 program was eliminated in FY2012. The FY2014 request for the NRT is $55.1 million.

government-wide GRF program. The Senate report asks NSF to work with OSTP on "how NSF could implement a broader program for graduate and undergraduate programs across the entire Federal Government, and to identify which programs across Government could benefit from such a program."[100]

The FY2014 NSF request seeks to shift certain programs between E&HR divisions and would merge the Mathematics and Science Partnership (MSP) and Computing Education for the 21st Century (CE21) programs. The merged program would be called, "Science, Technology, Engineering, Mathematics, including Computing Partnerships (STEM-C Partnerships)." The FY2014 request for STEM-C is $57.1 million. The Senate report accepts the proposed change to these programs and provides $57.1 million for STEM-C Partnerships.

Other E&HR accounts in the FY2014 budget request include Advanced Technological Education (ATE, $64.0 million), Robert Noyce Scholarship (Noyce, $60.9 million), and CyberCorps: Scholarships for Service (SFS, $25.0 million). The explanatory statement (as adjusted to reflect the rescissions, but not sequestration) provided $67.6 million for ATE, $53.8 million for Noyce, and $44.1 million for SFS in FY2013. Both House and Senate reports provide the requested level for ATE. The Senate report provides $60.9 million for Noyce and $45.0 million for the SFS program. The Senate report also provides the FY2012 level for the Advancing Informal STEM Learning (AISL) program ($61.4 million). The House report directs NSF to continue disseminating the findings of a report on best practices in STEM education and to develop methods to track and evaluate the implementation of recommendations from that report.

Selected broadening participation programs from the FY2014 request include Historically Black Colleges and Universities Undergraduate Program (HBCU-UP, $31.9 million), Tribal Colleges and Universities Program (T-CUP, $13.3 million), Louis Stokes Alliances for Minority Participation (LSAMP, $45.6 million), and Centers for Research Excellence in Science and Technology (CREST, $20.2 million). The explanatory statement (as adjusted to reflect the rescissions, but not sequestration) provided $32.3 million for HBCU-UP, $13.1 million for T-CUP, $46.8 million for LSAMP, and $24.5 million for CREST in FY2013. The House and Senate reports provide the requested level for HBCU-UP and LSAMP. The House report also provides the requested level for T-CUP; the Senate report provides $190,000 more. The Senate report also provides the requested level for CREST and for the Alliances for Graduate Education and the Professoriate (AGEP, $7.8 million).

The FY2014 request for the MREFC account is $210.1 million. NSF indicates that this amount would provide a final year of funding for the Advanced Interferometer Gravitational-Wave Observatory (AdvLIGO) and Ocean Observatories Initiative (OOI), as well as the first year of funding for the Large Synoptic Survey Telescope (LSST). Funding for the Advanced Technology Solar Telescope and National Ecological Observatory Network (NEON) would continue. The House report provides an amount ($182.6 million) that is equal to the funding request for continuing projects, but that would not cover costs of the first year of construction for the LSST. The Senate report provides the requested level and welcomes the start of LSST construction.

The Administration seeks $304.3 million, $4.5 million, and $14.3 million, respectively, for AOAM, NSB, and OIG in FY2014. After the rescissions (but before sequestration) P.L. 113-6 provided $293.2 million, $4.3 million, and $13.9 million, respectively, for these accounts in

[100] S.Rept. 113-78, p. 124.

FY2013. The House report provides $294.0 million for AOAM; the Senate report provides about $5.0 million more.

The FY2014 NSF budget request also includes funding for three multi-agency initiatives: National Nanotechnology Initiative (NNI, $430.9 million), Networking and Information Technology Research and Development (NITRD, $1.227 billion), and U.S. Global Change Research Program (USGCRP, $326.4 million).

Table 12. NSF Funding by Major Account, FY2013 and FY2014

Budget authority in millions of dollars

Account	FY2013 Enacted (Before Sequestration)	FY2014 Request	FY2014 House Committee Reported	FY2014 Senate Committee Reported	FY2014 Enacted
Research and Related Activities	$5,859.2	$6,212.3	$5,676.2	$6,018.3	
Biological Sciences	n/s	(760.6)	n/s	n/s	
Computer and Information Science and Engineering	n/s	(950.3)	n/s	n/s	
Engineering	n/s	(911.1)	n/s	n/s	
Geosciences	n/s	(1,393.9)	n/s	n/s	
Mathematical and Physical Sciences	n/s	(1,386.1)	n/s	n/s	
Social, Behavioral, and Economic Sciences	n/s	(272.4)	n/s	n/s	
Office of Cyberinfrastructure[a]	n/s	—	n/s	n/s	
Office of International Science and Engineering[a]	n/s	—	n/s	n/s	
U.S. Polar Programs[a]	n/s	—	n/s	n/s	
Integrative Activities[a]	n/s	(536.6)	n/s	n/s	
U.S. Arctic Research Commission	n/s	(1.4)	n/s	n/s	
Education and Human Resources	877.0	880.3	825.0	880.3	
Major Research Equipment and Facilities Construction	192.1	210.1	182.6	210.1	
Agency Operations and Award Management	293.2	304.3	294.0	298.4	
National Science Board	4.3	4.5	4.1	4.5	
Office of the Inspector General	13.9	14.3	13.2	14.3	
Total: NSF	**7,239.8**	**7,625.8**	**6,995.1**	**7,425.9**	

Source: FY2013-enacted (before sequestration) and FY2014-requested amounts are from S.Rept. 113-78. The FY2013-enacted amounts include the rescissions specified in Sections 3001 of the Consolidated and Further

Continuing Appropriations Act (P.L. 113-6) and the rescissions ordered by OMB pursuant to Section 3004 of the act. The FY2013-enacted amounts also include supplemental appropriations for the CJS departments and agencies included in the Disaster Relief Appropriations Act, 2013 (P.L. 113-2). The House committee-reported amounts are from H.Rept. 113-171 and the Senate committee-reported amounts are from S.Rept. 113-78.

Notes: "n/s" means "not specified." CRS was unable to identify a defined amount of funding for this account. Numbers are rounded.

a. On September 7, 2012, the NSF announced that it was realigning four directorates within the Research and Related Activities account. This transition was scheduled for October 1, 2012. Under the new account structure, the Office of Cyberinfrastructure was to become a division within the Directorate for Computer and Information Science and Engineering. The Office of Polar Programs was to become a division within the Geosciences directorate. The Office of International Science and Engineering and the Office of Integrative Activities were to be merged to become the Office of International and Integrative Activities. NSF indicates that these changes to the foundation's account structure have been made.

Related Agencies

The related agencies received a total of $870.1 million under the Consolidated and Further Continuing Appropriations Act. For FY2014, the Administration requests a total of $962.1 million for the related agencies. The House Committee on Appropriations recommends $800.5 million for the related agencies while the Senate Committee on Appropriations recommends $962.1 million.

Table 13. Funding for Related Agencies, FY2013 and FY2014

Budget authority in millions of dollars

Commission, Office, or Corporation	FY2013 Enacted (Before Sequestration)	FY2014 Request	FY2014 House Committee Reported	FY2014 Senate Committee Reported	FY2014 Enacted
U.S. Commission on Civil Rights	$9.2	$9.4	$8.8	$9.4	
Equal Employment Opportunity Commission	362.3	372.9	355.0	372.9	
International Trade Commission	82.8	85.1	79.0	85.1	
Legal Services Corporation	358.4a	430.0	300.0	430.0	
Marine Mammal Commission	3.0	3.4	2.9	3.4	
Office of the U.S. Trade Representative	50.2	56.2	50.0	56.2	
State Justice Institute	5.0	5.1	4.8	5.1	
Total: Related Agencies	**871.0**	**962.1**	**800.5**	**962.1**	

Source: FY2013-enacted (before sequestration) and FY2014-requested amounts were taken from S.Rept. 113-78. The FY2013-enacted amounts include the rescissions specified in Sections 3001 of the Consolidated and Further Continuing Appropriations Act (P.L. 113-6) and the rescissions ordered by OMB pursuant to Section 3004 of the act. The FY2013-enacted amounts also include supplemental appropriations for the CJS departments and agencies included in the Disaster Relief Appropriations Act, 2013 (P.L. 113-2). The House committee-reported amounts were taken from H.Rept. 113-171 and the Senate committee-reported amounts were taken from S.Rept. 113-78.

Note: Amounts may not add to totals due to rounding.

a. This amount includes $1.0 million in supplemental funding for the Legal Services Corporation.

Commission on Civil Rights

Established by the Civil Rights Act of 1957, the U.S. Commission on Civil Rights (the Commission)

- investigates allegations of citizens who may have been denied the right to vote based on color, race, religion, or national origin;

- studies and gathers information on legal developments constituting a denial of the equal protection of the laws;

- assesses the federal laws and policies in the area of civil rights; and

- submits reports on its findings to the President and Congress when the Commission or the President deems it appropriate.

P.L. 113-6 provided $9.2 million for the Commission. The Administration requests $9.4 million for the Commission for FY2014. The House Committee on Appropriations recommends $8.8 million for the Commission while the Senate Committee on Appropriations recommends $9.4 million, the same as the Administration's request.

Equal Employment Opportunity Commission (EEOC)[101]

The Equal Employment Opportunity Commission (EEOC) enforces several laws that ban employment discrimination based on race, color, national origin, sex, age, or disability. In recent years, appropriators were particularly concerned about the agency's ability to reduce the pending inventory of charges due to rising caseloads and limited staff. Due to new hires of enforcement staff and developments in technology, the EEOC continues to reduce the pending inventory of cases.

The Consolidated and Further Continuing Appropriations Act included $362.3 million for the EEOC. The Administration's FY2014 request for the EEOC is $372.9 million, which includes $29.5 million for payments to state and local entities with which the agency has work-sharing agreements to address workplace discrimination within their jurisdictions (i.e., Fair Employment Practices Agencies, FEPAs, and Tribal Employment Rights Organizations, TEROs). The House committee-reported bill would provide $355.0 million for the EEOC. The Senate Committee on Appropriation recommends $372.9 million for the EEOC.

The pending inventory of private sector cases filed with the EEOC reduced from 78,136 at the end of FY2011 to 70,312 at the end of FY2012, a 10% decline.[102] According to the EEOC, the decline reflects investments in staffing, training, and technology.

The EEOC federal sector hearings workload reduced from 8,847 in FY2011 to 8,687 hearings in FY2012.[103] The EEOC continues to implement strategies to reduce both federal and private sector

---

[101] This section was prepared by Abigail Rudman, Information Research Specialist, Knowledge Services Group, Domestic Social Policy Division.

[102] FY2014 Equal Employment Opportunity Commission, Congressional Budget Justification, Chart 2. Private Sector Charges Pending at Year End for Fiscal Year 2010 to Fiscal Year 2016, http://www.eeoc.gov/eeoc/plan/2014budget.cfm

[103] FY2013 Equal Employment Opportunity Commission, Congressional Budget Justification, Chart 7: Federal Sector (continued...)

cases by implementing a new case management system as outlined in the EEOC Strategic Plan for FY2012-FY2016.

U.S. International Trade Commission (ITC)[104]

The U.S. International Trade Commission (ITC) is an independent, quasi-judicial agency established by Congress that advises the President and Congress on U.S. foreign economic policies. In its *Strategic Plan* for 2009-2014, the ITC identified the following five strategic operations, which define the functions of the agency: (1) import injury investigations, (2) intellectual property-based imports investigations, (3) industry and economic analysis, (4) tariff and trade information services, and (5) trade policy support.[105] As a matter of policy, its budget request is submitted to Congress by the President without revision. The Consolidated and Further Continuing Appropriations Act provided $82.8 million for the ITC. The Administration's FY2014 request for the ITC is $85.1 million. The House committee-reported bill would provide $79.0 million for this account. The Senate Committee on Appropriation recommends $85.1 million for the ITC.

Legal Services Corporation (LSC)[106]

The Legal Services Corporation (LSC) is a private, nonprofit, federally funded corporation that provides grants to local offices that, in turn, provide legal assistance to low-income people in civil (noncriminal) cases. The LSC has been controversial since its incorporation in the early 1970s and has been operating without authorizing legislation since 1980. There have been ongoing debates over the adequacy of funding for the agency and the extent to which certain types of activities are appropriate for federally funded legal aid attorneys to undertake. In annual appropriations bills, Congress traditionally has included legislative provisions restricting the activities of LSC-funded grantees, such as prohibiting any lobbying activities or prohibiting representation in certain types of cases.

Although the authorization of appropriations for the LSC expired at the end of FY1980, the LSC has operated for the past 33 years under annual appropriations laws.

P.L. 113-2, the Disaster Relief Appropriations Act, included $1 million in disaster assistance for LSC-funded programs to provide aid to low-income people in areas significantly affected by super storm Sandy. P.L. 113-6 provided a total of $357.4 million for the LSC for FY2013.

For FY2014, the Obama Administration requested $430.0 million for the LSC. The Administration's FY2014 budget request includes $400.3 million for basic field programs and required independent audits, $19.5 million for management and grants oversight, $3.5 million for client self-help and information technology, $4.2 million for the Office of the Inspector General,

---

(...continued)

Appeals Workload Fiscal Year 2010 to Fiscal Year 2016, http://www.eeoc.gov/eeoc/plan/2014budget.cfm

[104] This section was written by M. Angeles Villarreal, Specialist in International Trade and Finance, Foreign Affairs, Defense, and Trade Division.

[105] U.S. Office of Management and Budget, *The President's Budget Fiscal Year 2012 Appendix, Other Independent Agencies, U.S. International Trade Commission*, p. 1249.

[106] This section was prepared by Carmen Solomon-Fears, Specialist in Social Policy, Domestic Social Policy Division.

$1.5 million for a new Pro Bono Innovation Fund, and $1.0 million for loan repayment assistance. The Obama Administration also proposed that LSC restrictions on class action suits and attorneys' fees be eliminated.

The House Committee on Appropriations recommends $300.0 million for the LSC for FY2014. This recommendation includes $271.9 million for basic field programs and required independent audits, $17.0 million for management and grants oversight, $3.4 million for client self-help and information technology, $4.2 million for the Office of the Inspector General, $2.5 million for a Pro Bono Innovation Fund, and $1.0 million for loan repayment assistance.

The Senate Committee on Appropriations includes $430.0 million for the LSC for FY2014. This recommendation includes $400.0 million for basic field programs and required independent audits, $19.5 million for management and grants oversight, $3.5 million for client self-help and information technology, $4.5 million for the Office of the Inspector General, $1.5 million for a Pro Bono Innovation Fund, and $1.0 million for loan repayment assistance.

Marine Mammal Commission (MMC)

The Marine Mammal Commission (MMC) is an independent agency of the executive branch, established under Title II of the Marine Mammal Protection Act (MMPA; P.L. 92-522). The MMC and its Committee of Scientific Advisors on Marine Mammals provide oversight and recommend actions on domestic and international topics to advance policies and provisions of the Marine Mammal Protection Act. As funding permits, the Marine Mammal Commission supports research to further the purposes of the MMPA.

The MMC received $3.0 million under P.L. 113-6. For FY2014, the Administration requests $3.4 million for the MMC. The House committee-reported bill includes $2.9 million for the MMC. The Senate committee-reported bill would provide $3.4 million for the MMC.

Office of the U.S. Trade Representative (USTR)[107]

The Office of the U.S. Trade Representative (USTR), located in the Executive Office of the President, is responsible for developing and coordinating U.S. international trade and direct investment policies. The USTR is the President's chief negotiator for international trade agreements, including commodity and direct investment negotiations. USTR also conducts U.S. affairs related to the World Trade Organization. The USTR is leading the negotiations for the United States for the ongoing talks for the proposed Trans-Pacific Partnership agreement (TPP) and for the Transatlantic Trade and Investment Partnership (T-TIP). The Consolidated and Further Continuing Appropriations Act provided $50.2 million for the USTR. The Administration's FY2014 request for this account is $56.2 million. The House committee-reported bill recommends $50.0 million for this account. The Senate Committee on Appropriation recommends $56.2 million.

---

[107] This section was written by M. Angeles Villarreal, Specialist in International Trade and Finance, Foreign Affairs, Defense, and Trade Division.

State Justice Institute (SJI)

The State Justice Institute (SJI) is a nonprofit corporation that makes grants to state courts and funds research, technical assistance, and informational projects aimed at improving the quality of judicial administration in state courts across the United States. It is governed by an 11-member board of directors appointed by the President and confirmed by the Senate.[108] Under the terms of its enabling legislation, SJI is authorized to present its budget request directly to Congress, apart from the President's budget.

P.L. 113-6 provided $5.0 million for SJI. For FY2014, the Administration requests $5.1 million for SJI. For FY2014, the House Committee on Appropriations recommends $4.8 million for SJI. The Senate committee-reported bill would provide $5.1 million, the same as the Administration's request.

Table 14. Funding for CJS Agencies, by Account, FY2009-FY2013

Budget authority in millions of dollars

Bureau or Agency	FY2009 Enacted	FY2010 Enacted	FY2011 Enacted	FY2012 Enacted	FY2013 Enacted (Before Sequestration)
Department of Commerce					
International Trade Administration	$420.4	$446.8	$440.7	$455.6	$461.4
Bureau of Industry and Security	83.7	100.3	100.1	101.0	99.7
Economic Development Administration	312.8	347.0	283.4	457.5	220.1
Minority Business Development Agency	29.8	31.5	30.3	30.3	28.1
Economic and Statistical Analysis	90.6	97.2	97.1	96.0	98.2
Census Bureau	3,139.9	7,324.7	1,149.7	888.3	905.0
National Telecommunications and Information Administration	39.2	40.0	41.6	45.6	45.0
U.S. Patent and Trademark Office	2,010.1	2,016.0	2,090.0	2,706.3	2,872.4
Offsetting Fee Receipts USPTO	-2,087.0	-1,887.0	-2,090.0	-2,706.3	-2,872.4
National Institute of Standards and Technology	819.0	856.6	750.1	750.8	807.1
National Oceanic and Atmospheric Administration	4,365.2	4,788.5	4,588.0	4,893.7	5,320.2
Departmental Management	83.8	107.5	99.8	88.9	85.0
DOC Subtotal	**9,307.5**	**14,269.2**	**7,580.9**	**7,807.7**	**8,069.8**
Department of Justice					
General Administration	2,067.8	2,285.8	2,208.1	2,227.9	528.5
General Administration	(370.8)	(456.9)	(312.2)	(262.1)	(141.3)
Administrative Review & Appeals	(266.0)	(298.8)	(296.1)	(301.0)	(303.0)

---

[108] By law, the President must appoint six state court judges, one state court administrator, and four members of the public, no more than two of whom may be of the same political party.

Bureau or Agency	FY2009 Enacted	FY2010 Enacted	FY2011 Enacted	FY2012 Enacted	FY2013 Enacted (Before Sequestration)
Detention Trustee	(1,355.3)	(1,445.7)	(1,515.6)	(1,580.6)	—
Office of the Inspector General	(75.7)	(84.4)	(84.2)	(84.2)	(84.2)
U.S. Parole Commission	12.6	12.9	12.8	12.8	12.5
Legal Activities	2,918.2	3,108.3	3,177.3	3,187.2	3,149.9
General legal activities	(805.7)	(889.0)	(863.4)	(863.4)	(862.7)
United States Attorneys	(1,851.3)	(1,943.2)	(1,930.1)	(1,960.0)	(1,928.9)
Other[a]	(261.2)	(276.1)	(383.8)	(363.8)	(358.3)
U.S. Marshals Service	964.0	1,190.0	1,140.1	1,189.0	2,794.2
National Security Division	85.2	87.9	87.8	87.0	88.2
Interagency Law Enforcement	515.0	549.6	527.5	527.5	511.0
Federal Bureau of Investigation	7,336.2	7,922.5	7,926.3	8,118.0	8,104.6
Drug Enforcement Administration	1,959.1	2,053.4	2,015.6	2,035.0	2,009.4
Bureau of Alcohol, Tobacco, Firearms & Explosives	1,068.2	1,158.3	1,112.5	1,152.0	1,129.7
Federal Prison System	6,178.9	6,208.1	6,384.1	6,644.0	6,779.6
Office of Violence Against Women	415.0	418.5	417.7	412.5	407.9
Office of Justice Programs	2,066.6	2,283.5	1,697.9	1,616.3	1,592.8
Research, Evaluation, and Statistics	(220.0)	(235.0)	(234.5)	(113.0)	(124.4)
State and Local Law Enforcement Assistance	(1,328.5)	(1,534.8)	(1,117.8)	(1,162.5)	(1,116.8)
Weed and Seed	(25.0)	(20.0)	—	—	—
Juvenile Justice Programs	(374.0)	(423.6)	(275.4)	(262.5)	(273.7)
Public Safety Officers Benefits	(119.1)	(70.1)	(70.1)	(78.3)	(78.0)
Community Oriented Policing Services	550.5	791.6	494.9	198.5	217.9
OVW, OJP, and COPS Salaries and Expenses	195.0	213.4	186.6	—	—
DOJ Subtotal	**26,332.3**	**28,283.7**	**27,389.2**	**27,407.7**	**27,326.1**
Science Agencies					
Office of Science and Technology Policy	5.3	7.0	6.6	4.5	5.7
National Aeronautics and Space Administration	17,782.4	18,724.3	18,448.0	17,800.0	17,506.7
National Science Foundation	6,490.4	6,926.5	6,859.9	7,033.1	7,239.8
Science Agencies Subtotal	**24,278.1**	**25,657.8**	**25,314.5**	**24,837.6**	**24,737.2**
Related Agencies					
Commission on Civil Rights	8.8	9.4	9.4	$.2	9.2
Equal Employment Opportunity Commission (EEOC)	343.9	367.3	366.6	360.0	362.3
International Trade Commission	75.1	81.9	81.7	80.0	82.8

Bureau or Agency	FY2009 Enacted	FY2010 Enacted	FY2011 Enacted	FY2012 Enacted	FY2013 Enacted (Before Sequestration)
Legal Services Corporation	390.0	420.0	404.2	348.0	358.4
Marine Mammal Commission	3.2	3.3	3.2	3.0	3.0
U.S. Trade Representative	47.3	47.8	47.7	51.3	50.2
State Justice Institute	4.1	5.1	5.1	5.1	5.0
Related Agencies Subtotal	**872.4**	**934.8**	**917.9**	**856.6**	**871.0**
Total Appropriation	**60,790.3**[b]	**69,145.5**[c]	**61,202.5**[d]	**60,909.6**[e]	**61,019.2**[f]
American Recovery and Reinvestment Act	15,922.0	—	—	—	—

Source: FY2008-enacted amounts taken from the House Committee on Appropriations' Committee Print on the Omnibus Appropriations Act, 2009 (P.L. 111-8), Division B. FY2009-enacted amounts taken from H.Rept. 111-366. FY2010-enacted amounts taken from S.Rept. 111-229. FY2011-enacted amounts were taken from H.Rept. 112-169. FY2012-enacted amounts were taken from H.Rept. 112-284. FY2013-enacted (before sequestration) were taken from S.Rept. 113-78. The FY2013-enacted amounts include the rescissions specified in Sections 3001 of the Consolidated and Further Continuing Appropriations Act (P.L. 113-6) and the rescissions ordered by OMB pursuant to Section 3004 of the act.

Note: Amounts may not add to totals due to rounding. Amounts include all supplemental appropriations, except that the FY2009 amounts do not include appropriations pursuant to the American Recovery and Reinvestment Act (P.L. 111-5).

a. "Other" includes subaccounts for the Antitrust Division, Vaccine Injury Compensation Trust Fund, U.S. Trustee System Fund, Foreign Claims Settlement Commission, Fees and Expenses of Witnesses, Community Relations Service, and the Asset Forfeiture Fund.

b. This amount does not include $610.6 million in rescissions of unobligated balances.

c. This amount does not include $531.2 million in rescissions of unobligated balances included in P.L. 111-117; $111.5 million in rescissions of unobligated balances included in P.L. 111-212; $129.0 million in rescissions of unobligated balances included in P.L. 111-224; and $1.788 billion in rescissions of unobligated balance included in P.L. 112-6.

d. This amount does not include $2.416 billion in rescissions of unobligated balances.

e. This amount does not include $905.9 million in rescissions of unobligated balances.

f. This amount does not include $881.6 million in rescissions of unobligated balances.

Author Contact Information

Nathan James, Coordinator
Analyst in Crime Policy
njames@crs.loc.gov, 7-0264

Jennifer D. Williams, Coordinator
Specialist in American National Government
jwilliams@crs.loc.gov, 7-8640

John F. Sargent Jr., Coordinator
Specialist in Science and Technology Policy
jsargent@crs.loc.gov, 7-9147

Wendy H. Schacht
Specialist in Science and Technology Policy
wschacht@crs.loc.gov, 7-7066

M. Angeles Villarreal
Specialist in International Trade and Finance
avillarreal@crs.loc.gov, 7-0321

Daniel Morgan
Specialist in Science and Technology Policy
dmorgan@crs.loc.gov, 7-5849

William J. Krouse
Specialist in Domestic Security and Crime Policy
wkrouse@crs.loc.gov, 7-2225

Heather B. Gonzalez
Specialist in Science and Technology Policy
hgonzalez@crs.loc.gov, 7-1895

Kristin Finklea
Acting Section Research Manager and Specialist in
Domestic Security
kfinklea@crs.loc.gov, 7-6259

Eugene Boyd
Analyst in Federalism and Economic Development
Policy
eboyd@crs.loc.gov, 7-8689

Lisa N. Sacco
Analyst in Illicit Drugs and Crime Policy
lsacco@crs.loc.gov, 7-7359

Dana A. Shea
Specialist in Science and Technology Policy
dshea@crs.loc.gov, 7-6844

Ian F. Fergusson
Specialist in International Trade and Finance
ifergusson@crs.loc.gov, 7-4997

Abigail B. Rudman
Information Research Specialist
arudman@crs.loc.gov, 7-9519

Harold F. Upton
Analyst in Natural Resources Policy
hupton@crs.loc.gov, 7-2264

Carmen Solomon-Fears
Specialist in Social Policy
csolomonfears@crs.loc.gov, 7-7306

Linda K. Moore
Specialist in Telecommunications Policy
lmoore@crs.loc.gov, 7-5853

Key Policy Staff

Area of Expertise	Name	Phone	E-mail
Departments			
Department of Justice	Nathan James	7-0264	njames@crs.loc.gov
Department of Commerce	Jennifer D. Williams	7-8640	jwilliams@crs.loc.gov
Science Agencies	John F. Sargent	7-9147	jsargent@crs.loc.gov
Agencies and Policy Areas			
OJP, COPS, BOP, U.S. Marshals	Nathan James	7-0264	njames@crs.loc.gov
FBI, ATF, U.S. Attorneys	William J. Krouse	7-2225	wkrouse@crs.loc.gov

Area of Expertise	Name	Phone	E-mail
Juvenile Justice	Kristin M. Finklea	7-6259	kfinklea@crs.loc.gov
DEA, OVW	Lisa N. Sacco	7-7359	lsacco@crs.loc.gov
Trade-related agencies: ITA, ITC, and USTR	M. Angeles Villarreal	7-0321	avillarreal@crs.loc.gov
BIS	Ian F. Fergusson	7-4997	ifergusson@crs.loc.gov
EDA, MBDA	Eugene Boyd	7-8689	eboyd@crs.loc.gov
Telecommunications, NTIA	Linda K. Moore	7-5853	lmoore@crs.loc.gov
Census Bureau, ESA	Jennifer D. Williams	7-8640	jwilliams@crs.loc.gov
Patent and Trademark Office, NIST	Wendy H. Schacht	7-7066	wschacht@crs.loc.gov
Office of Science and Technology Policy	Dana A. Shea	7-6844	dshea@crs.loc.gov
NOAA	Harold F. Upton	7-2264	hupton@crs.loc.gov
NASA	Daniel Morgan	7-5849	dmorgan@crs.loc.gov
NSF	Heather B. Gonzalez	7-1895	hgonzalez@crs.loc.gov
Equal Employment Opportunity Commission	Abigail B. Rudman	7-9519	arudman@crs.loc.gov
Legal Services Corporation	Carmen Solomon-Fears	7-7306	csolomonfears@crs.loc.gov